This book is dedicated to the many photographers, known and unknown, who have left us a visual record of Fredericton's history.

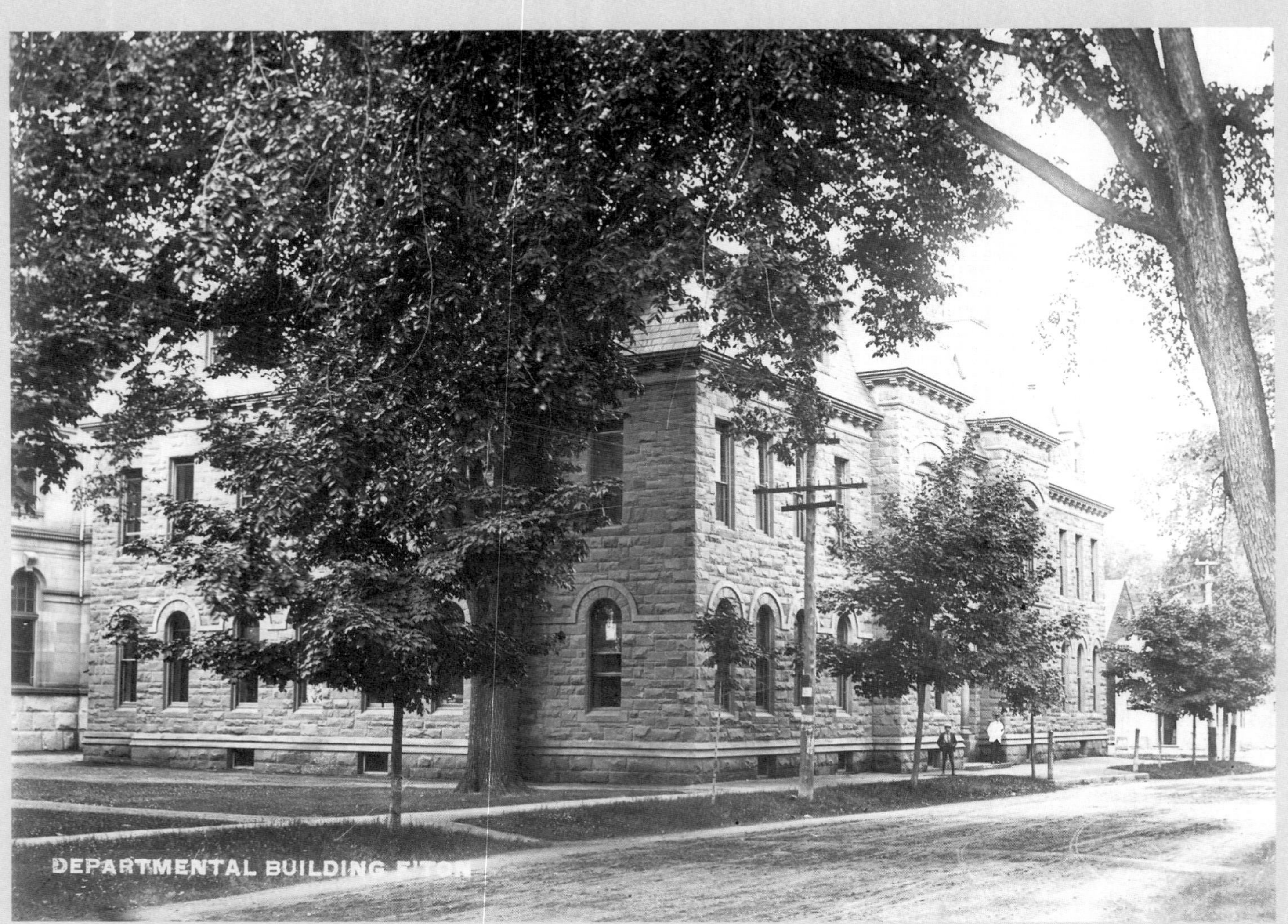
DEPARTMENTAL BUILDING

# CONTENTS

# A Halfpenny Map of Frederiction, 1878

Published in 1878, the Halfpenny Maps give valuable details about New Brunswick communities. This map of Fredericton shows the early streets and some of the major landmarks and estates.

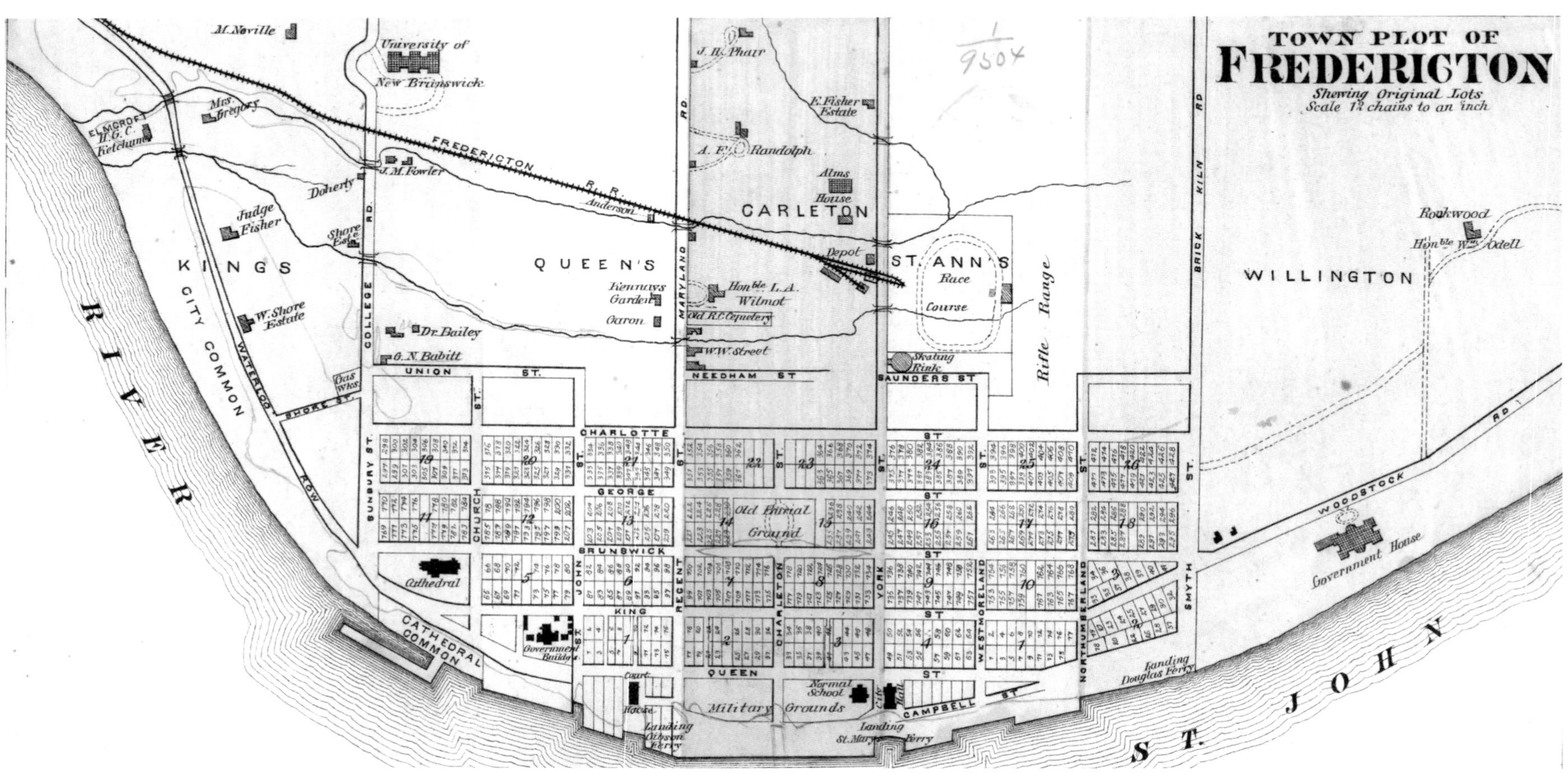

As most Fredericton-area school children know, the city's first long streets laid out parallel to the St. John River were named quite logically. Queen, King, Brunswick, George, and Charlotte streets honoured King George III of the House of Brunswick and his wife, Queen Charlotte. The names of the early cross streets—Regent, Carleton, York, and Smythe—also have historical significance. From 1811 to 1820, the eldest son of George III ruled as regent for his ailing father; Colonel Thomas Carleton (brother of Sir Guy Carleton) was appointed the first governor of the separate province of New Brunswick in 1784; the second son of George III was the Duke of York; and it was Governor Stracey Smyth who officially named the streets in 1819, some 35 years after Lieutenant Dugald Campbell laid out the town. However, the story of the settlement of the area goes back much beyond the arrival of the United Empire Loyalists.

Over many centuries, the St. John River carved out a 450-mile course from its headwaters in the State of Maine to its mouth at Saint John, on the shore of the Bay of Fundy. As the river turned southwest about eighty miles from the sea, the current wore away the river bank on the north and built up a sizeable plain on the south. Behind the plain lay swamps and brooks and, behind these, hills. At this site, often referred to as St. Anne's Point in the seventeenth and eighteenth centuries, a series of communities developed over a period of several hundred years.

Maliseet tribes were familiar with the area long before the Europeans arrived. There are the remains of an old Maliseet burial ground just above Old Government House on Woodstock Road. When English settlers came to survey a townsite at St. Anne's Point in 1762, the Maliseets drove them farther down-river. When Lieutenant-Colonel Sir Isaac Allen was given a land grant at St. Anne's in 1786, he recognized the Maliseet claim by paying them compensation. In the mid-1800s, several Maliseet families began occupying land on the north side of the river opposite St. Anne's Point, and their descendants continue to live there today.

The first Europeans to set foot on the site of the future Fredericton were probably French, either missionaries or traders, with English and Scots coming soon after. While France controlled Acadia, Pierre de Joibert, Sieur de Soulanges et Marson, received three seigneuries along the St. John River. One, at "Nachouac" (Nashwaak), was about six miles long on each side of the river and six miles deep inland. This land grant would have included most of modern-day Fredericton. It later passed to Louis d'Amours.

In 1690 Chevalier Robineau de Villebon was appointed governor of Acadia. After establishing himself at Fort Jemseg, in 1692 he built Fort St. Joseph, often referred to as Fort Nashwaak, on d'Amours' seigneury. The fort had some 45 occupants, including a small garrison of 40 soldiers, and served as a centre for attacks by the French and Indians on English settlements in New England. Villebon's successor, de Brouillon, destroyed Fort Nashwaak after 1698 on orders from France.

In 1713 the Treaty of Utrecht gave Acadia to Britain. Since France claimed that the land north of the Bay of Fundy was not part of Acadia, there was some Acadian settlement in the St. John valley, despite the negative impact of flooding along the river in the spring.

St. Anne's Point appears to have been settled in about 1732. In 1733 there were some fifteen French families, a total of 82 persons, living on the site of what is now Fredericton. The population swelled briefly after the expulsion of the Acadians in 1755, and there was a village, including a chapel and several hundred acres cleared, near the site of Old Government House. After the fall of Louisbourg to the British in 1758, General Monckton made plans to destroy French settlements along the St. John River. In

February 1759, soldiers led by Lieutenant Moses Hazen destroyed houses, barns, and cattle; St. Anne's Point was left a blackened ruin.

In the 1760s, the St. John's River Society, a group of men living in various British American colonies, was formed to obtain land grants in the lower valley, with a view to making profits from the venture. Two of their five land grants included most of the area of present-day Fredericton and more: Sunbury (125,000 acres) extended from Mill Creek (near what is now Wilsey Road) to Longs Creek, on the southern bank; Newtown (40,000 acres) extended from Maugerville upriver for eight miles, on the northern bank. Because many of the grantees did not meet the government's requirements for settling the land, most of it reverted to the government.

By 1765 John Anderson had established a trading post on the site of Fort St. Joseph, and he obtained a grant of one thousand acres on both sides of the Nashwaak River.

An enumeration early in 1783 listed 51 people at St. Anne's Point and Newton, and 334 Acadians (some perhaps from a large group that had set out from Boston in 1766) above St. Anne's Point at such places as Aukpaque or Aucpac (now Springhill), Douglas, and Keswick.

During 1783, more than 14,000 United Empire Loyalists arrived in New Brunswick in the aftermath of the American Revolution. They came in three groups—the Spring Fleet, the Summer Fleet, and the Fall Fleet. About two thousand travelled upriver to St. Anne's Point. A few settlers arrived by late summer and had time to build log huts. Most, however, arrived at Salamanca, at the lower end of St. Anne's, late in October, and found no individual lots surveyed and few provisions made for them. Snow fell on November 2, and an early freeze-up of the river prevented adequate food supplies from reaching them. Most of these Loyalists spent the winter in tents banked with snow and covered with spruce boughs as their only protection against the bitter cold. Many died and were buried beside the river.

In March 1784, the survivors sent a request to Governor Parr at Halifax that a town be laid out at St. Anne's Point. On June 21, 1784, the British government made Nova Scotia north of the Bay of Fundy into a separate province named New Brunswick. During that summer, a townsite, to be named Osnaburg and extending from Mill Creek to present-day University Avenue, was surveyed. In February 1785, the new governor, Colonel Thomas Carleton, ordered a survey of a town at St. Anne's Point, to be called Frederick's Town in honour of the king's second son; the name was gradually shortened to Fredericton.

In 1788, Carleton (by then referred to as lieutenant-governor) decided to move the capital from Saint John to Fredericton, near the head of tide and also the farthest point to which sailing ships could safely travel up the St. John River. He felt that this change would speed up the settlement of lands in the centre of the province; the site was also less vulnerable to attacks by sea. The Legislative Assembly met for the first time in Fredericton on July 18, 1788.

Almost as soon as the Loyalists had built themselves homes, wood being the most popular material, they made provision for the education of their children. The Provincial Academy of Arts and Sciences, which eventually developed into a college and then a university, was established in 1785.

By 1802 the Legislative Assembly was able to meet in the newly constructed Province House; after the wooden structure was destroyed by fire in 1880, the current stone legislative building was erected and ready for use in 1882. After the governor's Mansion House, built by Thomas Carleton, was damaged by fire in 1825, construction began on the stone residence called

Government House, first occupied in 1828. The York County Gaol was built about 1842 and the York County Court House in 1855.

A military presence was an integral part of life in Fredericton from the arrival of the Loyalists until after Confederation. When the town was first laid out, instructions had been given to set aside an area in the centre for the garrison and other buildings. The Artillery Park Barracks came first, at the corner of George and Regent streets. The Ordnance Stores occupied six lots between Queen and King streets, just below York Street. The barracks were built in 1784 and 1798.

The stone Soldiers' Barracks in the Military Compound was built in 1826-1827, and construction began on the nearby stone Officers' Quarters (replacing a wooden section damaged by fire in 1834) in 1839, with additions and renovations continuing into the 1850s. The wooden wing near Queen Street was torn down in 1925. The wooden Guard House, destroyed by fire in 1825, was replaced by a stone one in 1828. An addition was built to the rear of the adjacent wooden Militia Arms Store (built in 1832) in 1884 to create a military hospital to replace the stone hospital, which was dismantled in 1876 to make way for the Provincial Normal School.

In 1846, Carleton Street, which had previously given access to the King's Wharf on the bank of the St. John River, was closed to public use. It was re-opened in 1885 to connect to Fredericton's first highway bridge.

In 1884, fifteen years after the departure of the British troops, an infantry school was established in the Military Compound, and a new drill hall was built in 1885. The purpose of the school was to provide high-quality training for leaders who could then train militia officers and men during the summer and winter.

Meanwhile, Fredericton had seen considerable growth in churches, with many current congregations tracing their beginnings to the 1790s onward. The predominant church was the Church of England, which by 1854 had 32 clergymen throughout the province. As a result, New Brunswick was made a separate diocese and Reverend John Medley was appointed bishop. Fredericton was chosen as the see and the site of the cathedral. According to ecclesiastical law, the centre of the see must be a city. Consequently, Queen Victoria sent letters patent, dated April 25, 1845, changing the town to the City of Fredericton; on March 30, 1848, the city was incorporated. Throughout much of the nineteenth century, the community was referred to as the celestial (heavenly) city because of the large number of churches.

The citizens, living in an area with a high proportion of wooden buildings, made provision for fighting fires by building a tank house, containing a water tank for that purpose, in 1823. That same year, an alms house was built at the back of town for the care of indigent persons. Fredericton got its first hospital for the use of citizens at large, through the efforts of Lady Alice Tilley, wife of Lieutenant-Governor Samuel Leonard Tilley. Opened in 1888, the wooden structure was first called Victoria Cottage Hospital and was incorporated in 1889.

The City Council decided in 1867 to build a combined city hall and market house at Phoenix Square. The structure was destroyed by fire in 1875, and the current city hall was built and was ready for occupancy in late 1876.

Fredericton continued to grow, with housing development spreading in all directions, including to the north side of the St. John River. An editorial in *The Capital* as early as March 1889 had suggested amalgamation of the city with Devon and Marysville, but it was not until 1945 that the town of Devon became part of greater Fredericton. Further expansion of the city boundaries would come later in the twentieth century.

Houses were built along tree-lined streets, avenues, and roads, and the arboreal canopy probably led first-time visitors prior to the 1950s to under-estimate the population of the "city of stately elms." The coat of arms bears the motto *Fredericopolis silvae filia nobilis*, identifying Fredericton as the "noble daughter of the forest." As the city continued to expand, an organized program of tree maintenance and replanting has allowed this feature to remain one of the attractions of the capital city.

## Sources Consulted for this Book

**Books and Booklets:** *The Story of Fredericton: Fredericton's 100 Years—Then and Now*; Helen Baker, *The Y's People*; H. Gertrude Davis, *The History of the Brunswick Street United Baptist Church*; D.W.F. Ganong, *A Monograph of Historic Sites in the Province of New Brunswick*; C.H. Gatchell, *Gatchell's Pocket Directory of Fredericton, 1886*; Isabel Louise Hill, *Fredericton, New Brunswick, British North America*; Jessie I. Lawson and Jean M. Sweet, *Our New Brunswick Story*; Lilian Maxwell, *The History of Central New Brunswick*; Arlee McGee and Mary Myles, *The Victoria Public Hospital, 1888-1976*; Edgar McInnis, *Canada*; Rev. William O. Raymond, *The River St. John: Its Physical Features, Legends and History from 1604 to 1784*; Kenneth Solway, *The Story of the Chestnut Canoe*; W. Austin Squires, *History of Fredericton: The Last 200 Years*; Slason Thompson, *Way Back Then: Recollections of an Octogenarian*; Robert L. Watson, *Christ Church Cathedral, Fredericton: A History*; Nellie Winters, *To Recall and Pass On*.

**Magazines and Periodicals:** *The Atlantic Advocate* (June 1983, May 1985); *The Officers' Quarterly* (1994-1997); *The Officers' Quarters* (1997-2000).

**Newspapers:** *The Daily Gleaner* (1889-1945, 2000-2001); *The Fredericton Evening Capital* (1881-1886), *The Fredericton Capital* (1886-1887), and *The Capital* (1887-1889); *The Head Quarters* (1856-1876); *The Morning Star* (1878-1879) and *The Star* (1879-1880); and *The New Brunswick Reporter* and *Fredericton Advertiser* (1844-1886).

**Archival Documents:** The Lilian Maxwell papers, the John A. Morrison papers, the George Taylor papers and family records, Census records, and various other sources.

## Fredericton's Early Photographers

Since the early 1800s, artists have recorded many aspects of Fredericton life in a variety of formats. Pencil and pen sketches, watercolours such as those of Bartlett, oil paintings, and lithographs have provided a pictorial history of the people, buildings, social events, and scenic views of the city. In 1860, an artist's drawing for *The Illustrated London News* portrayed the arrival of the Prince of Wales in Fredericton, for an international readership.

With the invention of the camera and various techniques for taking and processing pictures, local photographers were able to record with greater accuracy and frequency the people, places, and events of Fredericton's history.

George Thomas Taylor (1838-1913) has left a legacy of hundreds of photographs. Born in Fredericton, he was eager to learn, and borrowed English periodicals on photography from officers at the garrison. He worked with local portrait photographer David Lawrence, but was also to a large extent self-taught. Taylor's knowledge of astronomy, chemistry, and electricity allowed him to produce his own first daguerreotypes in 1856, using the silver-plate process created by Louis Daguerre in 1839. Taylor built his own cameras and other equipment, a particularly useful skill for a man who took picture-taking beyond his studio to the outdoors. He is credited with the invention of the blueprint. Taylor was a welcome visitor at Government House, which he was the first to photograph. He undertook a photographing tour of New Brunswick in 1863, at which time Lieutenant-Governor Arthur Hamilton Gordon gave him a letter of introduction to take on his first journey. He continued touring the province to take photographs until 1906.

Photographer George Taylor's letter of introduction, 1863

The Bearer Mr Taylor has been requested by me to take photographic views of various places in the province. I shall feel obliged to all those who afford him facilities for the prosecution of the labours he has undertaken.

Fredericton
Sept 7. /63.

Arthur H Gordon

Coffin's Daguerreotype Saloon advertised its services by 1851, and Tuck's Photo Saloon was in operation by the 1870s. In the late 1870s George A. Burkhardt established his photography business on Queen Street and produced pictures of local landmarks for commercial distribution, as well as taking many photos of individual people and groups in his studio. William A. Walsh worked as a photographer for Burkhardt, and later established his own studio. George W. Schleyer had a photography shop on Queen Street by the 1880s, and in 1883 he advertised that he had bought George Taylor's view (scenery) negatives.

John Harvey Jr. (1861-1901), born in Fredericton, decided as a teenager that he wanted to be part of the thriving photography business in the city. He travelled to New York to take two years of intensive artistic training and then returned to Fredericton in 1883, doing portraits on a small scale. In May 1884, he opened a new studio on Queen Street, just below the People's Bank. His shop had good lighting and up-to-date equipment, and he created a prosperous business. When he died in 1901 at age 39, his widow, Martha, assumed the ownership and operation of Harvey's Studio, with Walter Lister as manager.

In 1902, E.E. Mersereau opened his photography studio at the corner of Carleton and Queen streets, and H.F. Albright was advertising himself as a landscape photographer located on Carleton Street opposite the Methodist church. By 1910, C.H. MacLean moved his photo business from his Carleton Street location to Queen Street.

Frank T. Pridham, born in Prince Edward Island, came to New Brunswick at an early age to study photography with his uncle, Robert Pridham, in Sackville. After working at the Mersereau Studio in Chatham and the Crandall Studio in Moncton, he came to Fredericton in 1917 and purchased Harvey's Studio from Martha Harvey. The sale was made on condition that the Harvey name would remain in perpetuity, and this has been honoured. Pridham carried his photographic skill beyond individual and group photos taken in his studio, going into the community to record on film people, places, and events. He was a charter member and a president of the Maritime Professional Photographers' Association, and was recognized several times by the Professional Photographers of Canada for his ability to teach photography. Some thirty professional photographers got their start with him.

Miss E. Madge Smith, born in England, came to Fredericton with her family when she was a child. She showed interest in creative work as a girl, and for six years she worked with photographer Frank Pridham. After she left this position to open a small art shop, she continued to take pictures, mostly as a hobby. She provided a legacy of hundreds of photos of Fredericton's scenery, buildings, special events, people, and local life.

Photographers such as Isaac Erb from Saint John and J.Y. Mersereau from the Miramichi visited Fredericton from time to time, and they added a further dimension to the pictorial history of the capital city.

The photographs in this book describe Fredericton from 1825 to the World War Two years, and within the limits of the original town plat—from Mill Creek to Phillis (Phyllis) Creek.

Chapter 1

# Military Compound

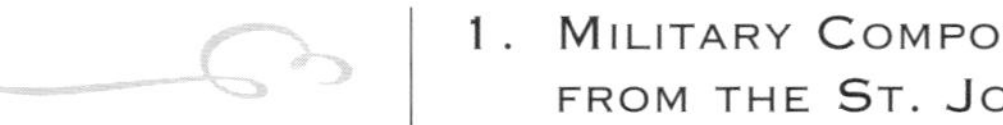

## 1. Military Compound as seen from the St. John River

A drawing of the Military Compound as seen from the St. John River. The Officers' Quarters (wooden and stone) is at the left, and the Soldiers' Barracks is in the centre, with the Guard House just to the right of the barracks and next to the Militia Arms Store. All four buildings are still standing.

2. Architect's plans for the stone Soldiers' Barracks, Fredericton.

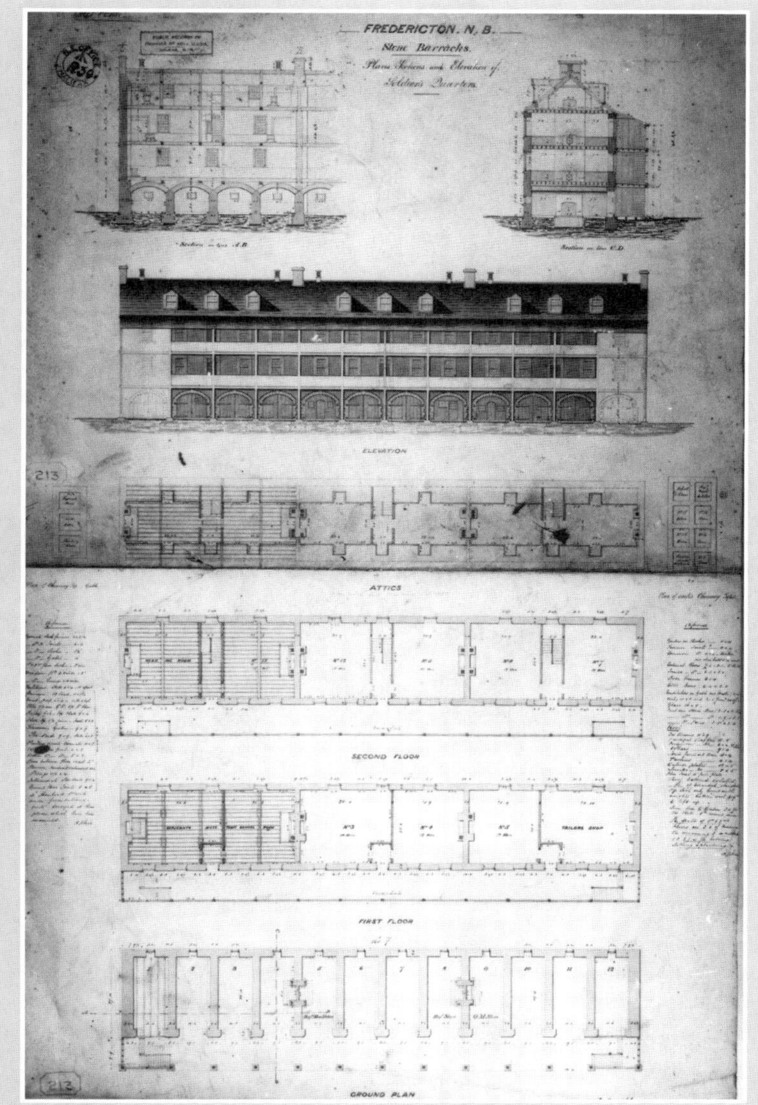


3. Architect's plans for the stone Officers' Quarters, Fredericton.

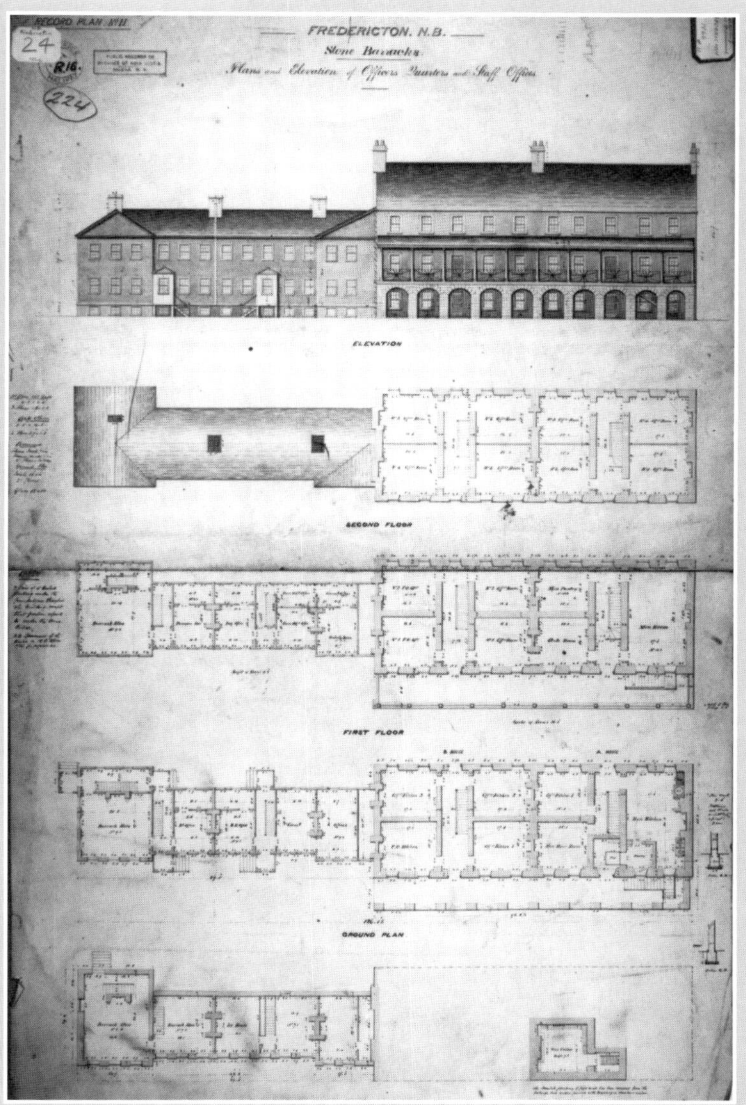

# 4. "Officers' Barracks at Fredericton, Winter 1834"

"Officers' Barracks at Fredericton, Winter 1834," from a sketch made by a Captain Campbell, son and aide-de-camp of the lieutenant-governor. The end of the barracks toward the river was destroyed by fire on April 16, 1834.

OFFICERS' BARRACKS at FREDERICTON.
Winter 1834.

## 5. The Officers' Quarters near Queen and Regent Streets

OFFICERS SQUARE F'TON

The Officers' Quarters, with its wooden and stone sections, and the stone fence running along lower Regent Street. The first building, called "the Pavilion," housed married officers and their families and began as a wood and brick structure of four long sections stretching from Queen Street towards the old military line on the river bank. Constructed in 1792, it burned in 1815, but the brick partitions, basements, and chimneys were left intact and were incorporated into the second wood and brick structure, built in 1816. When fire struck again in 1834, the brick firewalls that projected two feet above the roof confined the destruction to the mess hall, kitchen, larder, pantry, waiters' room, and wine cellar in the section next to the river. By 1840 this part was rebuilt with stone, from plans sent out from the War Office in England. In 1853, part of the next adjoining wooden section was removed and replaced with stone. When the remaining wooden structure was demolished in June 1925, workmen removed an old timber bearing the chalk inscription "REBUILT 1816."

## 6. The interior of the Military Compound

mid-1800s

The interior of the Military Compound. The Guard House is the low stone building with pillars. Constructed in 1828, it contained an orderly room, a guard room, and detention cells. Near the well are the wash-house and the stone kitchen. The stone Soldiers' Barracks is at the right, and the wooden fence runs along Queen Street. The three-storey barracks was built in 1826-1827 to accommodate over two hundred men in three 19-bed rooms, nine 16-bed rooms, and six attic rooms. Two balconies on the river side of the barracks gave privacy and shade. Note the tall ladders, ready for use in the event of fire. In 1923, the building became a liquor warehouse, remaining so until World War Two.

# 7. The western end of the Military Compound

before 1876

The western end of the Military Compound, before the land was sold to begin construction of the Provincial Normal School in 1876. The stone building in the foreground is the two-storey Military Hospital. At the corner of Queen Street is the shop of tinsmith Napoleon LaForest, whose lease expired at the end of the year. LaForest remained in business, however, opening a new shop on Queen Street in June 1882. In the distance, at far right, the Soldiers' Barracks is visible.

## 8. Men of the 22nd Cheshire Regiment

1867

A group of men of the 22nd Cheshire Regiment, in front of the Officers' Quarters in 1867. Included in the photograph, from left to right, are: J. St.G. Wolsley, J. Collins, J. Hammersley, C. Chauncy, H. Leigh, J. Hughes, J. Busfield, F. Parry, A. Tatham, T. Tyacke, F. Welch, W.S. Cooke, G.A. Christian, H.C. Patton, and H. Norris. This regiment, which completed its three-year posting in 1869, was the last group of Imperial troops to be stationed in Fredericton. Accompanying the regiment on their journey from New Brunswick were eighty young brides from Fredericton.

The regiment left behind Private John Brennen, who had been brutally murdered in October 1868. Prior to their departure, the officers and soldiers erected an eight-foot marble monument over Brennan's grave in the St. Dunstan's Cemetery on Regent Street.

## 9. Imperial troops drilling at the race track

c.1866

Imperial troops drilling at the old one-mile race track in Fredericton, circa 1866. Known as The York Driving Park, it was apparently the only one-mile race track in the province at that time. By the 1880s, the grandstand had fallen into a neglected state, and the Fredericton Park Association was formed in November 1886 to remedy the situation. A new half-mile track, stables, and a grand-stand capable of seating nine hundred people were built.

Members of the Fredericton Rifle Company lined up in front of the York County Court House (at left) on Queen Street. This building was at one time the location of the military training school. Although these men were not part of the regular military force, they were trained and enthusiastic members of the militia, called upon to provide guards of honour, internal military service, and defence of the border. During the border dispute between Maine and New Brunswick in the 1820s and 1830s, the militia played an important role, travelling to the Woodstock and Grand Falls area via the new Royal Road. In December 1837, the Rifle Company attached to the First Battalion of the York County Militia relieved from duty the last detachment of the 43rd Regiment (stationed as the garrison at Fredericton) so it could proceed, with other detachments, to Upper Canada, where a rebellion was in progress. On August 4, 1860, the "York Light Dragoons" under L.A. Wilmot formed the escort for the visiting Prince of Wales.

The Fenian Brotherhood had been organized in New York in 1857 by a group of Irish Americans who wanted to fight for Irish independence. In addition to aiding attacks in Ireland and bombings in England, they hoped to gain support in North America for their cause. The massing of Fenian fighting forces along the borders of New Brunswick and Upper and Lower Canada posed a very real threat to the security of the British North American colonies, and the Fenians made some ineffectual raids across the border in the 1860s. The danger of armed attack also caused concern in England, which had been trying to reduce the size of colonial garrisons as the colonies won responsible government. Thus, the militia became more and more important.

The brick building at the right belonged to Thomas Rainsford.

## 11. Military officers at the militia training camp 1865

Military officers while camped at the one-mile race track in July 1865. They include Lieutenant-Colonel Andrew Otty (third from left), and then Lieutenant-Colonel Hurd Peters, Major W.T. Baird (from Woodstock), Captain E. Simonds (seated), Lieutenant-Governor Arthur Hamilton Gordon, Captain Hallowea (of the 15th Regiment, and probably ADC), Captain E.B. Bear (seated), Colonel Crowder or Colonel Anderson, and probably Captain Arnold (from Sussex). The New Brunswick government put on a 28-day training camp for 2,800 militia soldiers that summer.

## 12. Military officers at the training camp in July 1865

Territorial (militia) soldiers in civilian clothes taking instruction at the race-course camp, near the Exhibition Palace, in July 1865. A new Militia Law that year called for an annual camp of instruction of at least 15 companies of the active militia, for a period not to exceed 28 days; a volunteer had to perform 13 drills within six months in order to qualify for pay. Consequently, men arrived from downriver on the steamer *Sunbury* and from upriver on the *Highlander*, combining with Fredericton-area militia for the 28-day camp. Major W.T. Baird and Lieutenant-Colonel L.A. Wilmot were in charge of the two battalions formed, and Colonel Gray had charge of the Officers' Company.

# 13. The Soldiers' Barracks on Queen Street

after 1869

The Soldiers' Barracks on Queen Street, some time after the departure of the Imperial troops in 1869. The barracks housed the provincial teacher-training facility from 1870 to 1876, and later several local organizations, including the Women's Christian Temperance Union (WCTU). At that time a doorway was cut into the Queen Street side and an ornate portico was built; these can be seen in this photograph. In 1884 the federal government decided to establish an Infantry School in the compound. Among the renovations was the removal of the entrance facing Queen Street.

## 14. The Soldiers' Barracks
c.1900

The Soldiers' Barracks, with its large sun dial on the east gable (partially hidden by the trees). A projecting iron rod (gnomon) throws a shadow on the dial, indicating accurate local apparent solar time from 9 A.M. until 1 P.M. The photograph, taken c.1900, also shows the gate on the high wooden fence running along Queen Street. From 1846 to 1885, access between Queen Street and the river was closed; then Carleton Street was re-opened to connect with the new highway bridge. The tower of City Hall is visible above the trees at far left.

## 15. The Wooden Highway Bridge and Drill Hall

The wooden highway bridge and, at left, the Drill Hall built for the Infantry School Corps. Both were constructed in 1885. The wooden Drill Hall accommodated "A" Company of the Infantry School Corps, later the Royal Canadian Regiment, and the 71st York Regiment. After a fire in 1903, the Drill Hall was not rebuilt until 1906. By 1934, the facilities at the Drill Hall were too small and unsatisfactory for the five units of the non-permanent active militia comprising the Fredericton garrison at the time. So the city could maintain its position as one of the leading militia centres in the Maritimes, the government decided to build a $46,000, three-storey brick annex at the west end. On November 17, 1936, demolition began on the old wooden section, and a modern brick armoury was ready for occupancy in 1937. This photograph is by George A. Burkhardt.

## 16. The first South African contingent

c.1900

The first South African contingent in Parade Square by the Soldiers' Barracks. When the Anglo-Boer War began on October 11, 1899, Canada offered to equip and send military forces to assist England. Canadians responded enthusiastically to enlist in the Infantry Battalion consisting of eight companies. "G" Company chose 109 recruits from New Brunswick and Prince Edward Island, with 32 accepted at the Fredericton depot.

## 17. The 71st Battalion Band

mid-1890s

The 71st Battalion Band, photographed by Burkhardt Studios in the mid-1890s. Front row, left to right: Herb Doak, James Edney, John Edney, George Parker. Second row, left to right: Alley Doak, Leonard Fleet, Albert Perkins, conductor George Offen, a Mr. Webb, James Coy, William Clark, Kenneth R. Chestnut. Third row, left to right: George Winters, William Burtt, William Mills, Frank Cadwallader, George Haviland, Robert Donovan. Back row, left to right: Ned O'Brien, Fred Risteen, Langford Good, Herb Wilkes.

The Battalion Band and its "relief" band of fifes and drums were very popular in the city. They played for regular concerts, church parades, Empire Day programs, steamer excursions, Sunday School picnics, cornerstone-laying ceremonies, and the arrival of special guests. These engagements were a source of money for uniforms, instruments, and the conductor's salary; the Militia Department provided uniforms for military occasions only.

## 18. The 71st Regiment Band

1907

The 71st Regiment Band, popularly known as the Gin Band, photographed by George Burkhardt in 1907. Front row, left to right: Herbert Green, George G. Baxter, Robert Coombes, Walter E. Hanlon. Second row, left to right: C. Percy Edgecombe, Percy W. Doak, Herbert Marshal, assistant bandmaster Elbridge Davey, bandmaster James White, Clem Toner, James E. Marten, A. John Ryan. Third row, left to right: Arthur F. Wentworth, Arthur Baxter, John Donovan, Captain Percy A. Guthrie (in civilian clothes), John White, Arthur O'Donnell, J.W. Donovan. Back row, left to right: William Spiers, Dougall McCatherin, J. Roselle Sheahan, H.E. Dewar, William C. Jarvis, Ernest P. Ryan.

Although this was a military band, the members had to provide their own instruments and uniforms and had to pay the conductor's salary. Controversy over funding in 1902 led to one third of the band members withdrawing; they were given their discharge from the regiment, many with the hope of forming or joining one of the civilian bands.

CHAPTER 2

# GOVERNMENT

Government House, showing part of the circular driveway and hedges, as well as the vines started by Lieutenant-Governor Lemuel Allan Wilmot. The conservatory, built in 1874, is at right. The architect for the official residence was John Elliott Woolford (1778-1866), an artist, topographical draftsman, and architect, who was barrack-master general at the military headquarters in Fredericton for 36 years. He also designed the building for King's College (the Old Arts Building) and the York County Gaol on Brunswick Street. The vacant conservatory collapsed under the weight of snow in February 1894.

## 2. The interior of the Conservatory at Government house

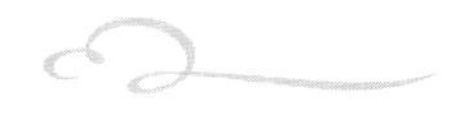

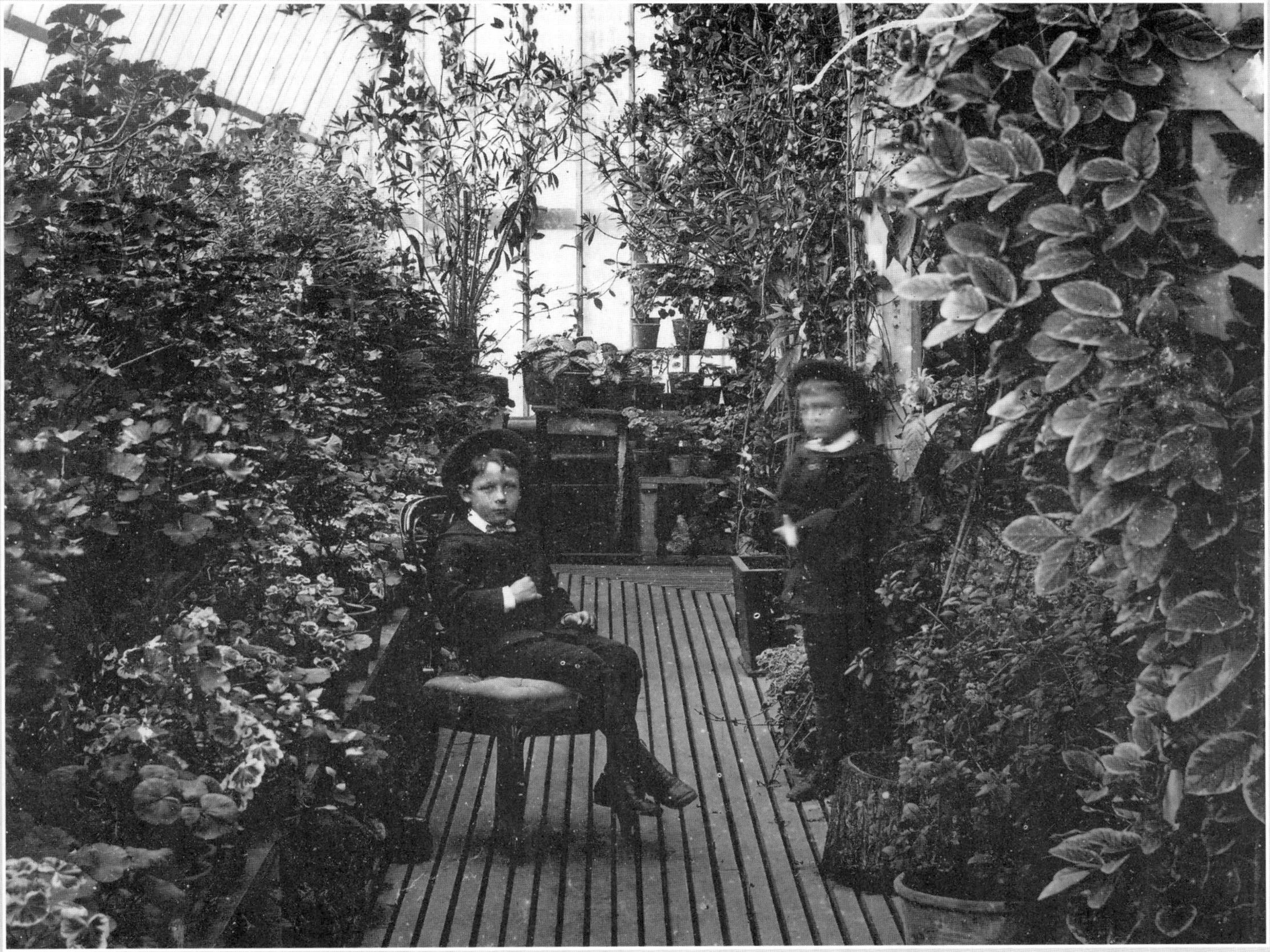

The interior of the conservatory at Government House. The two boys, Leonard P.D. and Herbert Tilley, are sons of Sir Leonard Tilley, the lieutenant-governor of New Brunswick (1873-1878 and 1885-1893). Sir Leonard was a delegate to the Charlottetown, Quebec, and London conferences that led to Confederation. His son Leonard Percy DeWolfe Tilley entered politics and was Conservative premier from 1933 to 1935.

## 3. Government House as seen from the St. John River

Government House, as seen from the St. John River. This is really the front of the residence, as the river was a major transportation route when the building was constructed in 1828. Government House was the scene of many state dinners and formal balls, the local newspapers listing the guests who attended. The New Year's levee was an annual event. Various dignitaries stayed here during official visits, including the Prince of Wales in 1860, whose second-floor bedroom (in centre) looked out on this garden. In August 1897, the furniture and furnishings were sold at public auction after the building ceased to be the vice-regal residence.

## 4. The front lawn of Government House, facing the river.

Croquet was often enjoyed on the lawn at Government House. During L.A. Wilmot's term as lieutenant-governor, the chief gardener for the property was Alexander Ross; Wilmot himself was also keenly interested in horticulture. James Berry had been Government House gardener from 1842 until 1867, when he left the position to start his own business. When Sir Leonard Tilley became lieutenant-governor in 1873, Berry returned and remained as gardener until his death in 1882, at which time the lieutenant-governor gave the job to Berry's son John.

## 5. Several gentlemen on the steps of Government House

The man in the light-coloured suit is Sir Arthur Hamilton Gordon, the last British appointee to serve a full term as lieutenant-governor of New Brunswick (1861-1866). He worked hard for Maritime Union and opposed the confederation of British North America. He travelled extensively throughout the province, and his book *Wilderness Journeys in New Brunswick* was published in Saint John in 1864. He went on to be governor of several other British colonies.

# 6. The King's American Coffee House

The frame house on lower Queen Street, built in 1788 as the King's American Coffee House. The first meeting in Fredericton of the provincial House of Assembly took place here on July 18, 1788. The photograph was likely taken by 1900.

A photograph of a lithograph by E.W. Bouvé, Boston, of Province House, centre, and public offices. Province House, built in 1802, was a large T-shaped building that housed the House of Assembly, Legislative Council Chambers, committee rooms for each of these, the Legislative Library, the Supreme Court and Law Library, and the office of the Registrar of Chancery. The government convened here until fire destroyed the building on February 25, 1880. The Provincial Secretary's Office, originally one storey, is to the left. It was not damaged by the 1880 fire, and a second storey and an attic were added before it came to be used as the Education Building. It is the oldest public building in Fredericton. The old Crown Land Office is to the right of Province House. In the background are the original Christ Church, built in 1794 near the site of the present Cathedral, and the Collegiate School.

## 8. The Legislative Assembly Building on Queen Street, opposite the Green

Officially opened in 1882 and for many years called the Parliament Building, the Legislative Assembly Building was built to replace the wooden Province House. J.C. Dumaresq designed the new building, which is 140 feet wide and 144 feet deep; the distinctive dome rises to a height of 144 feet. The foundation walls are faced with Spoon Island granite, and the exterior walls are of freestone from Dorchester. Cherry wood was used extensively for interior finishing. The Assembly Room, 45 by 55 feet, is 42 feet high and accommodates a visitors' gallery. A six-foot statue of Britannia with her trident, a symbol of Britain's dominance on the sea at that time, stands high above the main entrance. Inside the building is a handsome, self-supporting spiral staircase that so impressed a visiting Oscar Wilde that he wrote his name on the wall of the stairwell leading to the dome, a few months after the building was opened.

## 9. The Legislative Assembly chambers, Fredericton

Note the chandeliers and three large portraits. At left is a portrait by M.A. Shee of John Holroyd, Lord Sheffield (1735-1821), who successfully opposed plans to change the Navigation Laws in favour of the United States, in 1783. In the centre is a portrait in the style of Sir Joshua Reynolds of Queen Charlotte; a portrait of King George III, the reigning monarch when New Brunswick became a province, hangs out of view of this photo. At right is a portrait of Charles Grant, Lord Glenelg (1778-1866), who was Colonial Secretary from 1835 to 1839; in 1836 he turned over control of the Crown Lands of New Brunswick to the Legislative Assembly, which in turn agreed to finance the expenditures of government departments and courts—a step toward responsible government for the province.

CHAPTER 3

# CELESTIAL CITY

## 1. The east end of Christ Church Cathedral

Christ Church Cathedral, before July 1911, from the east end. Built under the direction of Bishop John Medley, it was modelled after a church in Snettisham, England, and was built primarily of New Brunswick materials. The architect was Frank Mills of Exeter, England, who came to Fredericton to supervise the building of the cathedral. In 1849, the year after he married the daughter of Archdeacon Coster, Mills moved to New York to set up his own office. (After his departure a number of changes were made in the original plan, as construction proceeded.) A red-pine hammerbeam roof over the nave and aisles was in place in 1849, and a decision was made to have one spire instead of two. The spire was erected in wood in 1851; its frame was constructed first on the floor of the cathedral, and was then taken apart and re-erected over the tower and covered in zinc. Butternut was used extensively for the interior furnishings, and many beautiful stained-glass windows were installed between 1850 and 1852. Eight years after its cornerstone was laid, it was consecrated on August 31, 1853.

## 2. Christ Church Cathedral after being struck by lightning

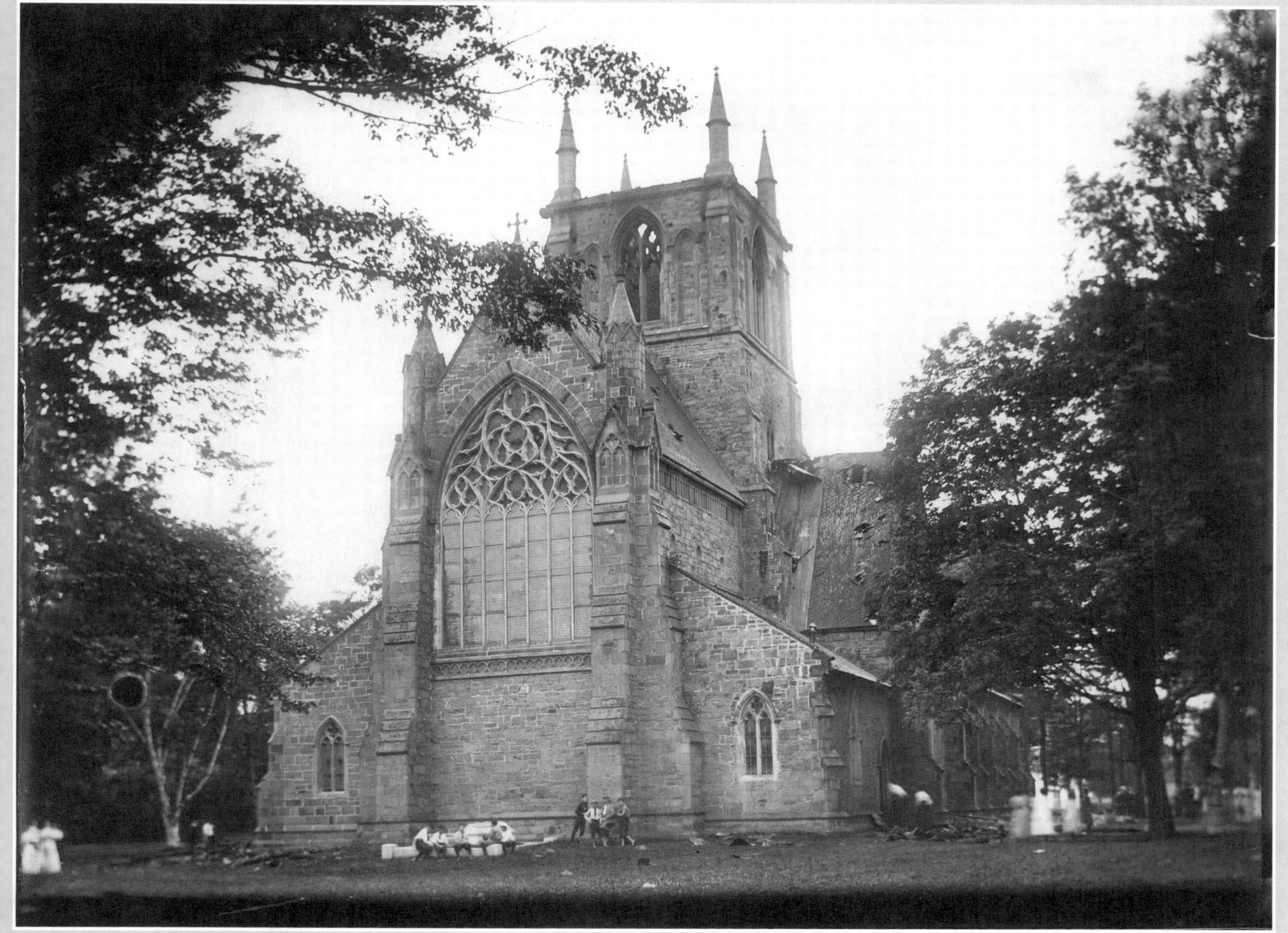

Christ Church Cathedral after lightning struck its south side on July 3, 1911. Fire spread quickly to the west gable, the roof, the tower, and the steeple. The 170-foot steeple crashed to the chancel floor. The eight bells melted and the new organ was destroyed. When the damage was repaired, the tower was reinforced and the steeple was built higher, to the intended height of 198 feet. Sir James Dunn gave a set of 15 bells to replace the eight lost in the fire. The restored cathedral was rededicated on August 24, 1912. The children at the front are seated on the tombs of bishops Medley and Richardson and their wives.

3. THE INTERIOR OF CHRIST CHURCH CATHEDRAL AFTER THE 1911 FIRE

## 4. The interior of Christ Church Cathedral, looking toward the chancel

Mrs. Margaret Medley presented a bronze altar cross in memory of her late husband, Canon Medley, son of Bishop Medley. It was an exact duplicate of one Canon Medley had designed for Norwich Cathedral in England. Three feet high, the cross was set with a garnet stone at each point and had four crystals on its base. It was dedicated on April 6, 1912. The east window, at the end of the chancel, was a gift from members of the Episcopal Church of the United States and from Mr. Wailes, the artist who designed it. Fortunately, there was no major damage to this window in the 1911 fire. The stone pulpit seen here at left, a gift of Mrs. Jane Hamlin Fellows, replaced the original butternut pulpit in 1911; the latter was shortened and sent to Trinity Church in Sussex.

5. Christ Church Parish Church, with its lych gate

Christ Church Parish Church (St. Anne's Chapel of Ease), showing the lych-gate at far right. Designed by English architect Frank Wills, under the direction of Bishop Medley, St. Anne's was consecrated on March 18, 1847, and is considered an excellent example of a North American parish church in the English Gothic Revival style. It provided rent-free pews to parishioners in the west end of the city. The lych-gate is a wooden structure with a roof and open sides, built at the entrance to a churchyard, to protect a coffin and its bearers from inclement weather as they waited for the arrival of the clergyman. St. Anne's is located at the corner of George and Westmorland streets.

6. The interior of Christ Church Parish Church, looking toward the chancel

The butternut pews have beautifully carved seat ends, and the floor is of Milton tile. A rood screen carved with three pointed Gothic arches and a high freestone ceiling arch separate the chancel from the nave.

Carleton Street, looking south, showing the rebuilt Methodist church, which had a dinstinctive wooden hand atop the steeple. An earlier church had been built on this site in 1830 to replace a smaller chapel near Westmorland and King streets. On November 11, 1850, eleven years after the church had been enlarged to seat six hundred people, the wooden landmark was destroyed by a disastrous fire that left almost every building between Carleton Street and Province Hall and as far back as Brunswick Street in ruins. Encouraged by Lemuel Allan Wilmot, an active member of the congregation, the members undertook construction of a much larger wooden church, designed by Matthew Stead of Saint John and dedicated on December 19, 1852. At Church Union in 1925, the church was renamed Wilmot United Church in honour of the man who had contributed so greatly in financial support and in serving for over thirty years as Sunday school superintendent and choir director. In the left foreground is the office of *The Farmer*, a newspaper published from 1863 under a number of slightly different names.

## 8. The interior of Wilmot United Church

The interior of Wilmot United Church, as seen from the rear balcony. Note the carved pulpit and three chairs on the dais, and the decorative front of the pipe organ. When the church opened in 1852, the choir and the organ were in the east gallery, behind the congregation. In 1881 a rounded addition was built on the west end, which provided space for a new pipe organ, installed in 1882. The choir, behind the pulpit, has sat facing the congregation ever since. The doors on the box pews are reminders of the days when the pews were sold and rented to specific members of the congregation.

New Brunswick became a separate Catholic diocese in 1842, with Fredericton as the episcopal see and Rev. William Dollard as bishop. This wooden structure was built in 1845 to replace the earliest Roman Catholic chapel, erected in 1824 by the first rector, Reverend Michael McSweeney. The chapel was moved to the rear and used as a parochial school until a church hall was built. A new bell was consecrated at St. Dunstan's Church on July 23, 1903. In 1858, during the pastorate of Rev. James McDevitt, a convent and rectory were built, and the Sisters of Charity came from Saint John. In 1870 the church purchased the hermitage property as a cemetery and later transferred remains from their Regent Street cemetery to the new one on the Woodstock Road. In 1887 *The Capital* newspaper announced that the church had purchased the Kenney property, on Regent Street near the railway track, in order to erect a new stone church since the current one was too small. On August 6, a "grand picnic" was held at Scully's Grove to raise funds, but a few weeks later the owner of the Kenney property changed her mind and the sale was cancelled. It would be many decades before a new St. Dunstan's Church was erected at the corner of Regent and Brunswick streets.

# 10. St. Dunstan's Roman Catholic Church

The interior of St. Dunstan's Roman Catholic Church, looking from back to front. Note the heating system of four stoves linked by overhead pipes.

The interior decoration of the church was done by Louis Rossa, a Swiss painter. The organ and choir were in the balcony at the back (south end) of the church. Signor de Angelis, bandmaster of the 76th Regiment, was choir director for several years, and his wife gave private singing lessons.

The "Auld Kirk," York and George streets, photographed by George A. Burkhardt. Built in 1830, it was incorporated in 1832 as a Presbyterian church. By the 1880s the congregation had outgrown the Kirk, which was moved to York Street to allow construction of a new stone church. The Kirk was moved again in about 1917, around the corner to Charlotte Street, to make room for the Fraser Memorial Building. Donald Fraser Sr. left a bequest for a hall for Sunday school and church auxiliary purposes. Built of Ashley granite and freestone, the three-storey structure was finished in fir and southern pine, with birch flooring. The plans included a gymnasium, an assembly room to seat six hundred, two dozen small rooms that could be closed off by folding doors, a kitchen, a kitchenette, and a small dining room. The building was dedicated on February 10, 1918. The old church at its Charlotte Street location was renovated into the Kirk Apartments.

## 12. St. Paul's Presbyterian Church

St. Paul's Church, at the corner of York and George streets. Built of stone and dedicated in 1886, St. Paul's replaced the "Auld Kirk," the original wooden Presbyterian church, which is the building with the cupola seen here. The church manse is at the left in this photograph. St. Paul's became part of the United Church of Canada in 1925. The plaque later placed by the Historic Sites and Monuments Board of Canada comments on its "High Victorian Gothic Revival" architecture, with its corner tower, intersecting roof ridges, and French Gothic rose window.

# 13. The wooden Baptist Church at York and Brunswick streets

The old Baptist Church at York and Brunswick streets, built in 1838-1840. The congregation was established in 1814 by Rev. Elijah Estabrooks and built its first meeting-house on King Street below Regent Street. The growing membership prompted the construction on York Street of the new and larger wooden church, dedicated on November 8, 1840. Rev. Charles Tupper, father of well-known politician Charles Tupper (Jr.), served as an itinerant minister there in 1825, and in 1838 was both the church pastor and the principal of the adjacent Baptist Seminary. In 1881 the church was raised, enlarged, and remodelled. After fire destroyed it on March 10,1882, reconstruction began on the same site. The new church, built of purple-blue and gray freestone and having an 80-foot steeple atop a 60-foot tower, was dedicated on November 11, 1883. In 1927 a new red brick building was added to provide classrooms for the Sunday School (established in 1822), a gymnasium, and improved kitchen facilities. The church became Brunswick Street United Baptist Church in 1905.

## 14. George Street Baptist church

George Street Baptist church, at the corner of York and George streets. After the 1858 decision to build a Free Baptist church, finances had to be procured. A fund-raising "tea meeting" was held, including a musical program and a wide variety of fine speakers, such as Dr. Hiram Dow (a well-known dentist), Rev. G.A. Hartley (from Saint John), Rev. Dr. Hurd, Rev. J.T. Parsons (from Marysville), Rev. Dr. Charles Spurden (from Brunswick Street Baptist Church), and Judge L.A. Wilmot. The new church was dedicated in 1861. Until a baptistry was added in 1882, all baptisms were conducted in the St. John River. The congregation joined the United Baptist Church in 1905. The church building was renovated into apartments in the 1960s.

## 15. The old Salvation Army barracks on King Street

Built circa 1885

The local Salvation Army, established in 1884 by Major Maltby, first met in the Temperance Hall on York Street, and then in a building at Queen and York streets. A fire in 1893 led to the construction the next year of a new citadel on King Street below Westmorland.

## 16. St. Andrew's Presbyterian Church on Charlotte Street

The congregation of St. Andrews was organized in 1925 by Presbyterians who did not wish to join the new United Church of Canada. Sunday services were held temporarily in the Capitol Theatre. Mrs. Archibald (Eliza Jane) Jewett donated land on Charlotte Street for a church; designed by architects Alward and Gillies of Saint John, the brick church with an attached hall was built by Forbes and Brown of Fredericton, at a cost of $68,400. It was dedicated on June 24, 1928, and was the recipient of many gifts. Pews were provided by the Senior Guild, and the communion table by the Young People's Society. Lady Ashburnham presented a lecturn and communion linen and, in later years, a silver tea service (bearing the family crest) from her husband's estate in England. Misses Janie and Jeanette Beverley bequeathed their family home, Grape Cottage (at 346 Brunswick Street), as a manse. Many memorial windows honour dedicated members of the congregation.

CHAPTER 4

# EDUCATION

## 1. The Baptist Seminary on York Street

opened on January 1, 1836

Although it was built by the Education Society for Baptist youth and others in the province excluded from the Collegiate School, when the Baptist Seminary opened more than half of the seventy students were non-Baptist. It operated as a boarding school, with twelve students' rooms on the second floor, while the main floor had a large hall, two classrooms, and the principal's apartments; a kitchen, dining room, and steward's apartments were in the basement. Renovations were made in 1872. When the Free Schools Act was passed in 1871, the seminary was sold to the newly formed Fredericton School Board, which operated it until it was replaced by a new brick school in 1891. During the construction period, the wooden building was moved to the corner of the lot and was later demolished. To the right in this picture are the stone Brunswick Street Baptist Church and the home of Dr. G.C. VanWart.

## 2. York Street School

BUILT IN THE EARLY 1890s

York Street School, built on the site of the Baptist Seminary to accommodate both elementary and high-school grades. From 1925, it housed elementary classes. The three-storey brick building, designed by J.C. Dumaresq and H.H. Mott of Saint John, had four spacious classrooms on each of the first two levels, and two additional classrooms and a large assembly hall on the top floor. Majestic granite steps graced all three outside entrances. The installation of electric lights in 1911 and an electric bell system were considered progressive additions. In 1923-1924, a new hardwood floor was installed in the assembly hall. During the school's 32-year history as a high school, 925 graduates have moved through its elegant arched hallways. Dr. Berton Caleb Foster was the only principal of the high school at this location, and the longest-serving one in Fredericton High School history.

3. CHARLOTTE STREET SCHOOL, OPENED IN 1885, WITH A CROWD OF STUDENTS OUTSIDE

In 1883 the Fredericton School Board learned that it could no longer rent classroom space in the Park Barracks at the corner of George and Regent streets, since the barracks was again needed for military purposes. All the other schools were filled to capacity, so arrangements were made to rent the upper flat of the first Cathedral Church Hall at the corner of Brunswick and Carleton streets until a new school could be built. A large lot on Charlotte Street was purchased, Saint John architects J.C. Dumaresq and H.H. Mott were hired, and Fredericton contractor Joshua Limerick was awarded the building contract. Construction began in the summer of 1884, and the two-storey brick school with its distinctive tower was finished a year later to provide education for children in the east end of the city. There were six large classrooms, each with a cloakroom and natural light from ten windows. Fine, quality oak wainscoting was used on the lower part of the walls, and the school was heated by three locally built wrought-iron furnaces in the full basement.

4. St. Dunstan's Hall on Regent Street, between King and Brunswick streets

Built in 1876, St. Dunstan's Hall was probably used as a Roman Catholic school until a new, two-storey school was opened on January 9, 1911. The new school, erected on the site of the first Catholic cemetery on Regent Street, was designed by Fredericton native F. Neil Brodie and was built of red brick (with free-stone trimmings) by Messrs. B. Mooney & Sons. It contained six classrooms and had a coal-fired furnace and good lighting and ventilation. The stone Knights of Columbus Hall stands at the left.

## 5. Fredericton High School on George Street, opened in 1925 at the site of the old Park Barracks

The school began in 1785 as the "Provincial Academy of Arts and Sciences," later the Collegiate School. Located near the river on lower Sunbury Street, it enrolled only Anglican boys and its teachers were Anglican clergymen. By 1793 a new schoolhouse was operating as a boarding school on lower Brunswick Street near the first Christ Church. Gradually the school became non-sectarian and, by the time it relocated to the York Street School, both boys and girls received instruction there.

The new high school was built at a cost of almost $160,000, with additional money needed to furnish it. This was all made possible by issuing voter-approved municipal bonds. The original brick building contained 23 classrooms, 13 rooms for vocational education, an assembly hall with a large, well-lighted stage and with space for 750 people, a gymnasium, a board room, a secretary's office, and private rooms for the principal and teachers. There were 425 students when the school opened for the fall term in 1925. As the school population grew, six classrooms were added in 1937, the first of several phases of expansion.

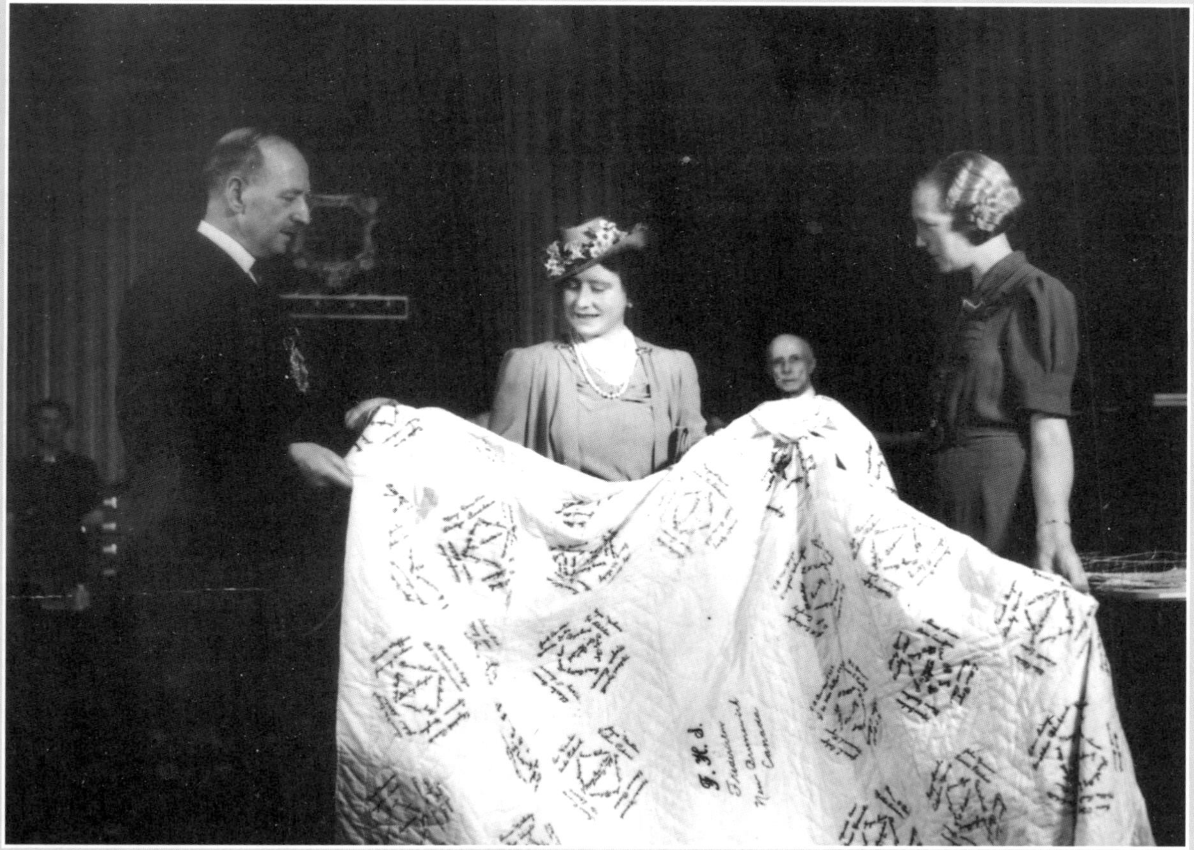

Her Majesty Queen Elizabeth (later the Queen Mother), admiring the Fredericton High School signature quilt, July 1941.The Lord Mayor of London is on the left. In order to assist the residents of Great Britain suffering the effects of German bombs during World War Two, an Air Raid Distress Fund was established, and "The Queen's Canadian Fund" was its national collecting agency in this country. Fredericton High School students responded enthusiastically to the appeal, and one of their projects originated with teacher Pearle Ross. Each student paid ten cents to write his/her signature in pencil on a yellow quilt block. The names were then stitched in black and assembled into a quilt that displayed the school colours. The head office of the fund in Montreal was so impressed by the quilt that they forwarded it to London.

# 7. King's College, forerunner of the the University of New Brunswick

King's College, seen from the bottom of the hill, with the gatekeeper's cottage and the small home of science professor Dr. James Robb in the foreground. The College of New Brunswick, given its charter in 1800, was re-structured as King's College and officially opened on January 1, 1829. Its new building, later called the Old Arts Building, was designed by John E. Woolford as a two-storey structure. It had forty-two rooms that accommodated twenty student dormitories, apartments for three professors and their families, servant quarters for the steward and his staff, classrooms, a refectory, a library, and a chapel. Today the building is known as Sir Howard Douglas Hall. To the left of the Old Arts Building is the Brydone Jack Observatory, built in 1851, the first in Canada. President Jack used it to determine the longitude of Fredericton.

# 8. The Old Arts Building

The Old Arts Building, decorated for its centenary in 1900. The third storey was added in 1876. Six Venetian poles, covered with red, white, and blue bunting, were placed at intervals in front of the college. The students hung festoons of greenery and flowers, along with banners, flags, and shields, from these poles. In 1860 the college became the University of New Brunswick and ceased to be an Anglican institution.

## 9. Women students at the University of New Brunswick

A group of women students on the steps of the Old Arts Building, 1905. Although women had been allowed to audit courses since the 1830s, it was not until 1886 that the university accepted women as students on an equal footing with men. Mary Kingsley Tibbits was the first female graduate, receiving a B.A. in 1889. By the time of this photograph, more than one hundred women had graduated from the University of New Brunswick.

## 10. The Library at the University of New Brunswick

The provincial government paid for the construction of this building of red and buff brick with sandstone trim. It was dedicated on May 12, 1931. The roof of the stone portico is supported by Doric columns, and the interior finish is simple and functional. The library was renamed the Bonar Law-Bennett Library when Lord Beaverbrook provided the money for a new wing on the uphill side, opened in 1951. Andrew Bonar Law has been the only Canadian-born prime minister of Great Britain, and R.B. Bennett, the only New Brunswick-born prime minister of Canada.

## 11. The Provincial Normal School

built in 1876-1877

The Provincial Normal School, seen from Phoenix Square. This building for teacher training was erected in 1876-1877 at the western end of the Military Compound. The land was acquired for $1,000 from the Dominion Government after lengthy negotiations. The three-storey structure was approximately 100 feet square, had brick walls on a freestone base and with freestone trim, and a slate roof. A model school (attended by city students below high school level for practice teaching) occupied the first floor until 1914, when a two-storey annex was built to house the Model School on the second floor and a gymnasium on the first.

## 12. A FRONT VIEW OF THE PROVINCIAL NORMAL SCHOOL

A front view of the Normal School, showing the main (Queen Street) entrance, framed in three Gothic arches supported by four red granite pillars. The pillars received slight damage during the 1929 fire, and may have been used again in the new school, which has a similar entrance design.

Johnny Rogers' class of grade seven and eight students at the Model School, in 1886.

## 14. The fire that destroyed the main building of the Normal School

May 5, 1929

A fire on May 5, 1929, began through spontaneous combustion of dust, waste paper, and other refuse in a wooden dust shute, and was fuelled by the extensive interior wood. By 5:30 P.M. only an empty shell—plus the two-storey annex that had been protected by a fire wall—remained. This photo was taken by W.H. Golden, whose confectionery shop was across from City Hall at the time.

# 15. The Coronation Parade honouring King George VI

May 12, 1937

Elaborate plans were made in Fredericton to celebrate the occasion of King George VI's coronation. City, provincial, and federal offices were closed, as were most businesses and stores. In the morning a community prayer service, in which the pastors of seven churches participated, was held at St. Paul's United Church, while Christ Church Cathedral had its own service. A royal salute was fired at noon by the 90th Field Battery, and a large parade left Queen's Square at 1:30, led by six RCMP members, militia units and men from the Carleton and York Regiment, and two batteries of the 12th Field Brigade. Floats on historical and patriotic themes prepared by schools, fraternities, organizations, and businesses, as well as the Knights of Pythias Band and members of the Devon and Fredericton fire departments, were part of the parade. On its route to the business district, the parade stopped at Parliament Square to listen over loudspeakers to the king's broadcast message. A coronation ball concluded the day's festivities.

The new Provincial Normal School is in the background of the photograph.

C H A P T E R 5

# Public Buildings

## 1. Fredericton City Hall

built in 1875-1876 at Phoenix Square

The City Hall built in 1875-1876 replaced the combined City Hall and Market House, which had burned on January 25, 1875. The new structure, built at a cost of $32,500 (raised by issuing debentures), measured 60 feet wide by 115 feet long. The basement was constructed of freestone, and the walls were faced with red brick and bands of freestone. At the main entrance, granite steps led to the porch, where red granite columns supporting the arches over the doorway rested on the marble-and-slate floor. The municipal offices and council chambers occupied the first floor. On the second floor was a public hall, known as the Opera House, which had a good stage and a horseshoe balcony. Able to seat about eight hundred, the Opera House was the entertainment centre of Fredericton until the late 1930s. The basement had four entrances and housed the farmers' market and, later, the Police Department.

## 2. The York County Gaol on Brunswick Street

Designed by John E. Woolford, the York County Gaol was built circa 1842, primarily of granite, with some field stone at the back. Here, a carriage passes while three uniformed officers stand in front of the building: John O'Neill, Zebedee Wright, and George Rideout (who later became chief of police in Moncton).

The old Post Office and Customs Building on the northeast corner of Queen and Carleton streets, possibly at its official opening on April 30, 1881. Built on public lands near the wharf and business district, the building was three years in the planning and construction phases, and cost about $25,000. The three-storey building had exterior walls of pressed brick, a foundation of rubble stone, and a mansard roof with a turret. The post office was on the ground floor, and had a service area with a wooden counter, two delivery wickets (one for gentlemen and one for ladies), and five hundred lock boxes, as well as a sorting area, the postmaster's office, and a money order, registry, and stamp office. The second and third floors accommodated the Customs and Inland Revenue Departments, which had another entrance on the west side. A separate brick building at the rear of the post office had facilities for the inspector of weights and measures.

## 4. The intersection of Queen and Carleton streets

CUSTOMS BUILDING AT LEFT—POST OFFICE AT RIGHT
QUEEN STREET

The intersection of Queen and Carleton streets, with the recently constructed post office (opened November 15, 1915) at the right. Note the dome with its clock faces. To the left is the customs house, its offices by then relocated to the ground floor. A branch of the Department of Agriculture moved into the offices on the second floor.

## 5. The Exhibition Palace, at Saunders and Westmorland Streets

Fredericton's Exhibition Palace, at the corner of Saunders and Westmorland streets. The city's desire to host the Provincial Exhibition prompted construction of this large, $28,000 building in 1864. Architect Matthew Stead designed it in the form of a Greek cross, with a large dome at the intersection of the four naves. The dome, 86 feet in diameter, was the largest piece of wooden framework ever raised in New Brunswick up to that time. On top stood a 20-foot-high glass cupola, topped by a 12-foot-high ornamental ball from which rose a 20-foot flagstaff. Corinthian pillars and life-size statues, representing the four seasons and the arts, science, agriculture, and shipbuilding, added to the elaborate exterior. A fence enclosed the cattle barn at right.

## 6. An interior view of Exhibition Palace

An interior view, from one balcony across to the other, of Exhibition Palace. There was a promenade on the main floor beneath the central dome, and four stairways led up to the gallery which ran around the entire building. Windows provided natural light in the daytime, and in the evening the building was lit with 650 gas-burning fixtures and with lamps held aloft by 24 statues.

## 7. The Exhibition Building constructed after 1877

The Exhibition Building, which replaced Exhibition Palace after it was destroyed in 1877 in a spectacular fire of uncertain origin.

# 8. Laying the cornerstone for the Victoria Cottage Hospital in 1887

Lady Alice Tilley, wife of the lieutenant-governor, laying the cornerstone for the Victoria Cottage Hospital on June 21, 1887, as part of the celebrations for Queen Victoria's Golden Jubilee. Inside the cornerstone was a letter from Queen Victoria, granting permission to use her name. At the ceremony there was a choir of more than five hundred children and adults, directed by Professor Bristowe. Lieutenant-Governor Samuel Leonard Tilley and Attorney-General Andrew G. Blair gave addresses. The bands of the Infantry School Corps and the 71st Battalion played, and the military troops were reviewed. A *feu de joie* was fired and a royal salute given.

# 9. Victoria Cottage Hospital

OPENED IN 1888, WITH LATER ADDITIONS

Victoria Cottage Hospital, the building at the centre, officially opened June 21, 1888, and was incorporated in 1889 as the Victoria Public Hospital. The three-storey wooden building had 14 beds, and its verandah and balconies allowed patients to get fresh air. Asa Dow of Canterbury donated money for the construction of facilities for patients with contagious diseases, so around 1889 the Asa Dow Isolation Wing was built to the west (left) of the hospital. In 1891 the extension to the right was constructed, with additions in 1901; by 1902 the hospital had 40 beds. In 1903 it received a bequest of $5,000 from the late A.F. Randolph, a prominent Fredericton businessman.

## 10. The Fraser Memorial Building at the Victoria Public Hospital

When lumber businessman Donald Fraser Sr. died in 1916, he provided a bequest of money to erect a new hospital building in front of the existing wooden structure. After a long delay because of building conditions, construction was under way by 1921, and local fundraising efforts began in order to assist in furnishing the new structure. Of the total cost of about $366,000, Mr. Fraser's sons, Archibald and Donald Jr., provided some $230,000; W.W. Boyce paid the entire cost (approximately $1,000) of building the connection between the old and new sections; and the city contributed $40,000 for the new power plant that was needed to run the hospital. Public subscriptions by organizations, churches, and individuals made up the rest. When the Fraser Memorial Hospital was officially opened on March 6, 1922, the three-storey building was considered one of the most up-to-date and well equipped hospitals in eastern Canada.

## 11. The Military Convalescent Hospital, on the old Government House grounds

The Military Convalescent Hospital buildings constructed on the grounds of Old Government House (visible in the background) in 1917-1918. On October 16, 1916, it was officially announced that Old Government House would become a convalescent home for returned soldiers after the Kelties 236th Regiment, then in barracks there, had left. The facility, to be called Unit K, was for soldiers in "class two"— still undergoing treatment but not yet discharged—and it was intended to provide treatment as well as retraining for men not able to return to their previous occupations as a result of their injuries. On September 18, 1917 it was announced that three additional structures would be added and connected to each other and to Government House by wide corridors. Three wooden units were built on the downriver side to accommodate hospital wards, recreational areas, dining rooms, kitchen space, quarters for the male and female help, and sun parlours at each end on both floors. Delays in getting building materials and equipment slowed construction, and it was late June of 1918 when the hospital began receiving patients. By that fall, the five hundred beds were fully occupied. In November 1919, with only one hundred patients, the facility ceased to be a hospital when it was handed over to the Department of Soldiers' Civil Re-establishment.

## 12. The Fredericton Water Works Pumping Station, on Smythe Street

The Station swas built in 1883-1884, when the city relied on the St. John River as its source of water. There was direct pumping, without any reservoir or stand-pipe, from a point at the most northerly part of the city at that time. Just over nine miles of piping were laid under the streets, at a cost of $85,000. The average pressure at the pump house was 35 pounds; when fires were being fought, the pressure was raised.

When the water works was installed, John M. Taylor, brother of photographer George Taylor, got a job firing the boilers. A mechanical genius without formal training, he studied the handbook that came with the pumping-house engine. When the hired engineer had trouble with the engine, Taylor quickly solved the problem. He was subsequently appointed chief engineer, a position he held until he was too old to work.

When improvements and alterations were made at the Pumping Station and Filtration Plant in 1912, City Council appointed C.L. Bowes as chief engineer, explaining that they could not find a properly qualified local man for the position.

## 13. The Central Hose Station No. 2 of the Fredericton Fire Department, on King Street

Seated on the wagons are Bill Wilson (left) and Steve Doucette (right). This wooden structure was erected in the 1870s, and originally had a bell tower at the front. The fire bell was rung from the ground with a rope. By the time this picture was taken, an electric fire alarm had been installed and the tower had been removed. At one time two steam fire engines, "The City of Fredericton" (often called the Silsby, after its manufacturer) and the "Alexandria," were stationed in this building.

In 1913, the fire department was temporarily relocated across the street while the old station was demolished and a new brick station was constructed on the same site. On September 30, 1914, a large reception and ball took place in the new building. The next day the fire department drivers and their families moved into their apartments in the fire station, and Chief Harry Rutter moved into his office there. Over the next few days, all the fire-fighting apparatus was moved into this new, central station.

## 14. No. 5 Hose Company
1895

Standing, left to right: Joe McMinniman, A. Blackmer. Seated, left to right: Lud McSorley, Johnston McKenzie, George Darlington.

## 15. Fredericton Fire Department No. 1 Hose Company

June 21, 1887

The men were wearing their uniforms as they prepared to join the procession to the cornerstone-laying ceremony for the new hospital. From left to right are John Tapley McLaughlin, Thomas Smith, Edward Segee, John Hersey, Nathaniel Smith, Isaac Burden, Edward McGinn, Henry Pollock, and Jack McGinn. The long ropes were used to haul the hose reel to fires.

## 16. A Fredericton Fire Department muster, 1931

A Fredericton Fire Department muster at the Central Station on King Street, October 4, 1931. Included in the photograph are two very important members of the force, fire horses Bill and Doll, who pulled either wagons or sleighs according to the season. Sitting at right on the wagon is driver Hugh ("Hoodie") O'Neill. Horses remained in service until February 1938, when a new fire truck arrived.

# 17. The Fredericton Police Force

ONE HUNDRED YEARS AGO

Left to right: John O'Neill, Paul Phillips, Zebedee Wright, George Rideout. The forage caps were similar to those of a railway conductor or a soldier's informal cap.

CHAPTER 6

# BUSINESSES

## 1. A VIEW OF QUEEN STREET, MIDWAY BETWEEN CARLETON AND YORK STREETS

The dry goods stores of John J. Weddall and of Tennant, Davies & Company, and the millinery shop of the Misses Young are opposite the normal school.

## 2. The interior of the Misses Young Millinery Store

c.1900

Sarah Grace Young, a graduate of the Normal School, left teaching and came to Fredericton, where she and her sister Eva (Eve) established this business around 1883. On February 24, 1886, Grace married Peter M. MacDonald, a clerk in the Tennant, Davies & Company store next door. The *New Brunswick Reporter* and *Fredericton Advertiser* wrote that bunting floated from the Tennant store in honour of the event. The MacDonalds built a large house on Waterloo Row and named it after his home in Scotland—Glen Isla; it was popularly known as Bonnet Hall. In this photo, Grace MacDonald is standing at the left in the shop, which employed up to ten milliners.

## 3. Queen Street, between Carleton and York streets

c.1930

From left are C.W. Hall Books and Stationery, Dominion Store (which came to Fredericton in 1929 as one of the early "chain" stores in the city), and Fred B. Edgecombe Dry Goods. At the far right is A.A. Belmore Dry Goods, which later moved above York Street. The tradition of May 1 being moving day for both families and businesses came to Fredericton from England and continued well into the 1900s. During April and May, newspapers carried advertisements of available houses and commercial premises, as well as notices of merchants' new locations. On April 27, 1912, *The Daily Gleaner* headed a small news item with "Many Residents Change Address on Moving Day" and listed the names of some prominent citizens and merchants who were moving.

## 4. Queen Street, looking west from Phoenix Square

At the left are W.H. Golden's Confectionery, Harvey's Studio, The People's Bank, and Fredericton Steam Laundry. When Sir Howard Douglas became lieutenant-governor in 1824, he advocated the establishment of savings banks, and several were set up in the 1820s and 1830s, with varying degrees of success. The People's Bank (with the pillared portico) was incorporated in 1864 and opened in 1865, with Archibald F. Randolph as its president. Conveniently located across the street from the Randolph wholesale grocery business, The People's Bank prospered, with an addition (which is still there with its rounded window) built on its upper side in 1901. In the days before houses and businesses had civic numbers, several stores and offices identified their locations as being next to, adjoining, the first door below, or opposite the People's Bank. In 1907, The People's Bank merged with the Bank of Montreal, operating at the same location until 1925, when a new building was erected at the corner of Queen and Carleton streets.

## 5. Queen Street above York Street
c.1900

Queen Street above York Street, with the new Chestnut Building, c.1900. The businesses from left are the R. Chestnut & Sons Hardware Store, the R.T. Mack Drugstore, and the American Clothing House. The Victoria Lodge IOOF and the law offices of Arthur R. Slipp had premises upstairs in the larger building. From 1935 to 1937 the YMCA rented space in the Chestnut Building, before moving to more spacious quarters in the Edgecombe Building at 88 York Street.

## 6. Queen Street, looking toward York Street

Queen Street above York Street with the Chestnut/ James S. Neill Hardware Store, National Shoes, W.H. Golden, and Harvey Studio. Robert Chestnut opened his hardware store in 1836, and incorporated it in 1858 as R. Chestnut & Sons. The store gradually expanded to sell many other types of products, including clothing and sporting goods. In 1924 Harry Chestnut, who had been managing the hardware store since his father's death in 1909, sold the business to competitor James S. Neill & Sons, a move that enabled Harry to give his full attention to the Chestnut Canoe Company. At the far left is Dibblee's Drug Store.

Lower Queen Street, with D.H. Crowley (confectionery and smokers' supplies), John G. Adams (undertaker), the Fredericton Board of Trade, and Confederation Life. This photograph was taken by the Walsh Studio. During the 1800s, carpenters and cabinet-makers often took on the additional roles of coffin-makers and undertakers, and companies would often place two types of advertisements, one promoting their furniture and another for their services for the bereaved. That there was competition is evident, as seen in Robert B. Adams's 1901 advertisement as the "Down Town Undertaker" and that of George W. Adams as the "Uptown Undertaker," along with a comparison of their prices and services.

## 8. Lower Queen Street, opposite the York County Court House

Lower Queen Street, with the James S. Neill & Sons Hardware Store at left and the Lemont & Sons Furniture Store at right, photographed by the Walsh Studio. The original location of the Neill Store was here, opposite the county courthouse. Ownership later passed to John Neill. In 1924 the Neills bought the Chestnut & Sons Hardware Store at the corner of Queen and York streets, and relocated to the Chestnut Building.

Soon after Martin Lemont came to Fredericton from the United States, he established a variety store that carried many types of stock, including furniture, crockery, fancy goods, and toys. In 1855 he imported the first kerosene oil ever used in Fredericton, and sold early oil-burning lamps. His first store was in the Slason building opposite Officers' Square. When this building was destroyed by the great fire of 1850, he relocated to Phoenix Square and, after another fire, to the Coy Block on Queen Street just below Regent Street. In 1871 he moved farther down Queen Street, to the location in this photo. His sons William and Martin Jr. formed a partnership with their father and, when the business became a joint stock company in 1905, grandson J.M. Lemont became president. By its 75th anniversary in 1919, Lemont's had become a house furnishings store, specializing in furniture, lamps, and floor coverings.

## 9. The Original Location of the Chestnut Canoe Factory

The original location of the Chestnut Canoe Factory, on the south side of King Street below Northumberland Street. Among the children at the right are Pearl, Ruby, and Thelma Delong, whose father, Harry Delong, is in the group of factory workers at left.

About 1897, the R. Chestnut & Sons Hardware Store put on display a canvas canoe built by the B.N. Morris Canoe Company of Veazie, Maine. Sons Harry and William Chestnut, great enthusiasts of outdoor sports, considered this new canoe to be of excellent design and quality. When Jack and Adam Moore, boat-builders with a shop at Phoenix Square, built a copy of this 18-foot canoe and had orders for others pour in, the Chestnuts offered to sell and help market any canoes the Moores built. An addition was built to the Chestnuts' King Street factory and, by February 1905, they had a modern building, complete with electric lighting and a gas engine. The Chestnuts owned the only canoe factory in Canada that built canoes using a wood and canvas construction, a technique for which they got a six-year patent.

The company was incorporated in August 1907, and a new factory (their third) was built on York Street. A fire in 1921 destroyed that factory, canoes, and valuable wood. When the factory was rebuilt, the company diversified, producing snowshoes and toboggans as well as canoes. Merging with the Peterborough Canoe Company under the name Canadian Watercraft Limited in 1923, the Chestnut Canoe Company continued to do business with the public under its own name. Eventually, Harry Chestnut's widow, Annie, sold the Chestnut shares to the Peterborough Company. After several more years of profitable business, changing technology and building materials would cause the Chestnut Company to close in the late 1970s.

# 10. Hoegg's Canning Factory on King Street

Hoegg's Canning Factory, operated by D.W. Hoegg & Co. Ltd. during the 1880s and 1890s. This factory, on King Street between Northumberland and Smythe Streets, was the third location at which the company did business. The factory canned tomatoes, locally grown vegetables, lobster, and various other foods.

Risteen & Co. Ltd. Sash and Door Factory, on upper Queen Street at Smythe Street. The front part of the structure is stone and was originally the Dibblee residence. After the house was damaged by fire, Joseph Risteen bought the property and converted it into a factory in 1872. J.C. Risteen was born in Fredericton but grew up on a farm in Carleton County. He came back to Fredericton to be apprenticed to a local carpenter for four years, lived several years in New York and Massachusetts, and then returned to New Brunswick in 1861, eventually setting up his business in Fredericton. When the company was incorporated in 1901 as J.C. Risteen & Company Limited, Henry, William, and Harry Chestnut were among the shareholders. In 1904-1905, when an addition was being built to the Chestnut factory, the Chestnuts used an upstairs section of the Risteen factory to build canoes. In this picture, a horse and sloven wagon can be seen at the side loading doors.

The West End Boat Livery, operated by William Calder, who died circa 1895. Mr. Calder had worked as a boat builder, carpenter, and carriage maker, at the corner of Westmorland and Campbell streets.

## 13. David Dunlap with his sloven wagon used to deliver ice

Ice was cut in the St. John River in winter and stored in sheds, with sawdust as insulation, for sale in summer. Sloven wagons had large wheels with crank axles that allowed the bed to ride low so large cargo objects could be handled more easily. An obituary in 1911 for long-time Fredericton grocery merchant James Hodge credited him with introducing the first sloven wagon to Fredericton, after he had seen the labour-saving vehicles used in Saint John.

## 14. John Bebbington's home, greenhouse, and gardens, on lower Charlotte Street

John Bebbington came to Canada from England in 1870 to become the gardener for Fredericton druggist J.W. Brayley, whose splendid gardens on his property at Westmorland and Brunswick streets provided lively competition at the Fredericton Exhibition with other avid gardeners such as L.A. Wilmot. In 1873 Bebbington was hired by John and Lucy Morrison to supervise the building of greenhouses and the laying out of grounds at Riverside, their property on the Lincoln Road. He was also responsible for the fine garden at Linden Hall, George Fenety's home. By 1876 Bebbington had started his own business on two lots of land on lower Charlotte Street. He not only provided an extensive variety of vegetable plants, flowers, shrubs, and trees, but also became the first local florist to create floral designs for funerals.

The Smith Foundry Company Ltd. on the south side of King Street between Carleton and York streets. Incorporated in 1911 by brothers Albert, Perry, and Harry Smith, the building occupied most of the block, with offices, a large machine shop, a moulding plant, and a paint shop. A later addition, The Fredericton Garage, sold the city's first automobiles, the Franklin and the MacLaughlin. During World War One, the foundry manufactured artillery shells, 24 hours a day, for the Canadian Army. After the war, the foundry returned to manufacturing industrial machinery and agricultural equipment, and operated until the mid-1930s.

# 16. The Hartt Boot & Shoe Company on York Street

The idea of building a shoe factory in Fredericton and using leather supplied by local tanneries was conceived in the mid-1890s by native-born Odbur M. Hartt. Construction of the building, designed by city architect William Minue, began in late 1898 and the boilers began to generate steam to operate the machinery on July 26, 1899. The staff, growing from 200 workers in 1899 to almost 500 in 1903, produced high-quality footwear, with daily production reaching 2,000 pairs by 1903. Under new management, in 1911 there were 160 employees with a monthly payroll of about $6,000; operating several nights a week as well as their day shifts, they had all the orders they could fill.

## 17. The original Board of Directors and management of the Hartt Boot & Shoe Company

December, 27, 1898

From left: Robert Savage (Business Manager), John Palmer (Vice-President), Odbur Hartt (Factory Manager), Edward Moore (Director), John Kilburn (President), Willard Kitchen (Director), James McCready (Secretary). Born in Fredericton, Hartt left at age 22 to work in the United States, where he became foreman and superintendent in several major shoe factories, acquiring a thorough knowledge of boot and shoe manufacturing. During summer visits home, he began to develop a plan for a factory in Fredericton, with proposed jobs for 300 local men and women. Hartt, his wife, and family returned to live in their native city, and in 1898 the company was incorporated. The directors, especially Hartt; his brother-in-law John Kilburn, a lumberman; John Palmer, a tanner; and Willard Kitchen, a merchant, brought a variety of skills and financial backing to the board.

## 18. Lower York Street, looking northeast
c.1886

Lower York Street, c.1886, with Edgecombe & Sons, carriage factory; Whittier & Hooper, commission merchants; and, on the corner, D.W. Estabrook, grocer. In 1840, John Edgecombe and Joseph Stentiford established a wagon and carriage business near Wilmot's Alley, on King Street. In 1852, the partnership ended, and each man set up his own business. "John Edgecombe, Manufacturer of Carriages, Waggons, and Sleighs," operated on York Street. He took several of his seven surviving sons (two had died) into the business, and by the 1870s, with 50 employees, it was the second largest factory of its kind in Canada and the only firm in New Brunswick that manufactured hearses. Despite having had several major fires since 1850, the Edgecombes won a gold medal at the Dominion Exhibition in 1890 for the company's collection of carriages and was recognized as one of the best firms in Canada. John Edgecombe, active in the business until age 81, died on December 18, 1890, without a will. The company experienced financial difficulties and internal family problems, and it closed its doors in 1898.

On January 21, 1936, a major fire (the worst since the 1929 fire at the normal school) gutted much of the four-storey building, destroying the Kenneth Staples Drug Store, the Beatty Appliance Store, and Turney Lee's Grand Cafe, and causing losses for Fred Leslie's grocery store, Ralph Shepherd's shoe repairing shop, and F. Emerson Edgecombe. The Edgecombe Building was rebuilt as a two-storey structure.

## 19. A salesman's carriage, built about 1888 by Edgecombe's Steam Carriage Factory

Alfred G. Edgecombe and his son Harold on King Street. After the Edgecombes relocated to York Street, there were five other carriage manufacturers in the 1880s along King Street, which was sometimes referred to as "Carriage Row."

This carriage was made for the St. Croix Soap Manufacturing Company of St. Stephen, New Brunswick, and promoted its all-purpose Surprise soap, suitable for toilet, bath, laundry, and scrubbing. Consumers were encouraged to save the soap wrappers; each person who sent 25 wrappers would receive a gift of a beautiful picture or a half-dozen Surprise lead pencils.

## 20. Arthur J. Ryan's Drug Store

c.1936

Arthur J. Ryan's Drug Store at the corner of Queen and Carleton streets, c.1936, photographed by C.H. McLean. This building was earlier occupied by druggist and apothecary W.H. Carten, whose estate still owned the building in 1911. Gradually it became known as the Ryan Building, a name which was retained after the wooden structure was sold, demolished, and replaced by a four-storey brick one. The building at the far left was used as a post office for many years before the post office at Queen and Carleton streets opened in 1881.

As a city in the midst of rich forests, Fredericton had numerous lumber and shingle mills, running on steam power, in the nineteenth and early twentieth centuries. The Victoria Mill, owned by Hale & Murchie, sawed long lumber exclusively, shipping much of it to the United States. In 1895, it had the largest "cut" of the local mills, with at least ten million feet of logs processed. In 1913, the Fraser Company completely remodelled the mill, making it one of the most modern band-saw mills in Eastern Canada. With over one hundred employees, it added the manufacture of shingles to its production.

The Aberdeen Mill, in the west end above Government House. Built in 1894 by the Fraser Lumber Company, the lumber mill, shingle and lath mills, and the box board business were destroyed in a spectacular blaze on August 12, 1905. The fire started beneath a clapboard machine on the first floor and spread so quickly that the approximately one hundred employees then at work barely had time to escape. The good firefighting equipment in the building was thus useless. The nearest fire hydrant was one-quarter mile away, and attaching sufficient hose lines was difficult. The city pumping station raised the water pressure from forty pounds to ninety, and efforts were directed at saving three cottages across the street and the company's large boarding house.

In 1917 Donald Fraser Jr., after personally supervising the reconstruction of the Aberdeen Hotel, including new plumbing and other renovations to make the structure perfectly sanitary, turned the building over to the Children's Aid & Protective Society. Citizens donated nearly all the furnishings, and each child had his/her own white iron cot. Various churches worked to provide the bedding for this new children's home, and bundles of clothing were donated. The society had the legal power to remove children from unhealthy or immoral situations and to place them in the home. The matron, Mrs. Troop, had ten children under her care when the home opened, and more were expected to arrive during the summer. The facility continued to operate until after World War Two.

## 23. Morrison's Mill, on the Lincoln Road

Photographed by George A. Burkhardt

Bought by John A. Morrison from Mr. Kilgour Shives in 1860, this mill shared a common problem with other wood mills—fire, with one occurring in 1860. In May 1872, not long after the mill had been refitted and put into operation for the season, fire broke out and destroyed it again. Fortunately, the engine and boilers were not seriously damaged, and none of the approximately 120 employees were thrown out of work, for Mr. Morrison promptly set about rebuilding. By September 3, the mill was back in full operation and it continued to prosper, despite another fire in 1885, after which a fourth mill was built on the site. In 1895, it sawed more than thirty million cedar shingles, even though dry weather and low water that summer caused delays in getting logs down the river. The mill was later purchased by the Phoenix Milling Company and then by the Fraser Company.

The area, which had a strong sense of community, was referred to as "The Mills." When lightning struck and set the local school on fire in July 1901, the school trustees promptly decided to rebuild. The burned building had accommodated 50 to 60 students in the half of the "quite old" structure that had been in use, and the former Temperance Hall was fitted up temporarily for school purposes by the opening of the term in late August. William Minue drew up plans for the new school; five years later he designed an additional storey and, in 1923, an annex for the school, to house a total of 125 students.

CHAPTER 7

# STREET SCENES

## 1. "Fredericton Fashionables, January 1834," a painting photographed by George Taylor in 1877

There is some question about the artist of "Fredericton Fashionables." Some say it was Lieutenant Campbell, a son of Lieutenant-Governor Sir Archibald Campbell; others say it was an original pencil sketch by a John Giles and that it hung in the Queen Hotel. The painting shows Phoenix Square, looking down Queen Street. From far left are the market hay scales, the Tank House, and a military lot (surrounded by a high fence) with the Soldiers' Barracks in the background. The Tank House contained a water tank for fighting fires, a Town Committee meeting room, and the general store of R.E. Burpé (whose name is over the door). The Officers' Mess, surrounded by a low fence, was across the street. The military owned all the lots on the south side of Queen Street below York, and eventually traded them for the current Officers' Square. At far right is the two-storey office of J.H. Drake, occupied much later by Neills' Hardware Store. Activity in Phoenix Square depicted here includes driving horses tandem, very popular among the elite until 1900. The people in the scene are said to portray particular individuals: the owner of the upset sleigh is Archdeacon Coster; the man with the dogteam is Mr. Louden, the local hangman; those in the sleigh across the foreground are William H. Odell and his sister; and the sleigh drawn by the four horses in the right foreground is Governor Campbell's.

## 2. A view of Queen and Regent streets as seen from Campbell Street c.1878

Note the gas lamp post at the left, the office of *The Morning Star* newspaper, and the fence enclosing the lawn at Officers' Square. Gas street lights began to be used about 1847. The Gas Company office was just below the County Court House, in the building that formerly housed the Bank of Fredericton in the 1830s.

The Commercial Hotel (H.B. Burden, proprietor) and L.R. Golding's Livery Stable are on the left, with the new City Hall in the distance. Edgecombe's Carriage Factory and Watson and Long's "F'ton Oyster Saloon" are on the right.

## 4. Queen Street, looking west

circa 1861-1873

J.H. Reid, Baxter's Confectionery, R. Anderson's Bakery, the City Bakery, and a shoe store (possibly Nelson Campbell's) are identified by their prominent signs. Fences such as the one seen along this dirt road were very common in Fredericton for the purpose of controlling roaming animals.

## 5. Market Square, later called Phoenix Square, with loads of hay for sale

c.1876

At left are the J. McNally Furniture Store, the S.L. Morrison Grocery Store, and the R. Chestnut Hardware Store. The ornate fence in the foreground still surrounds the normal school building. Hay was much in demand for the many cows and horses kept by Frederictonians. In July 1888, *The Capital* newspaper published a notice reminding citizens that there was a fine for leading or riding horses, cows, or other animals on sidewalks, pavement, or planked footpaths in the city except to cross the street. To the right are The Randolph Building and City Hall.

## 6. Upper Queen Street, looking east

The St. Stephen branch of the Loyal Orange Lodge takes its place as a procession forms in front of the Orange Lodge Hall. The celebration of the "glorious twelfth" each July marked the English victory at the Battle of the Boyne in 1690, after William of Orange had come at the invitation of the House of Lords to suppress Catholicism. Extensive plans were made in many Canadian cities to have religious services, large parades, and speakers, and Fredericton was no exception. Sometimes Orangemen from several communities would travel to one location in order to mark the day, which explains the presence of the St. Stephen branch in Fredericton on this occasion.

## 7. Lower Queen Street near Court House Square

At left are the harness shop of H. Rutter and the James S. Neill & Sons Hardware Store. Lemont's store stands near the centre. The white horse at the head of the procession suggests that this is a July 12 parade.

## 8. Phoenix Square, looking down Queen Street 1897

Phoenix Square, looking down Queen Street on Dominion Day of 1897, Queen Victoria's Diamond Jubilee. From far left can be seen spectators on the steps of City Hall, the first normal school, the post office (later the customs house), and the Soldiers' Barracks (above the trees). The decorated posts at the foot of the steps support coal-gas lamps. Bunting hangs from various businesses, including Lottimers, shoe store; Dever Brothers, dry goods; John J. Weddall, dry goods; John M. Wiley, pharmacy; Fred Edgecombe, dry goods; and Thomas W. Smith, merchant tailor. In addition to drugs, medicines, and toilet articles, Wiley also sold garden and field seeds provided by local nurseries such as Lucy Morrison's. The fountain in front of City Hall was built during the summer of 1885 through public subscriptions of $2000.

## 9. The intersection at Smythe, King and Brunswick streets

At the left is the west-end bandstand on the Smythe Street Green, built by the generosity of citizens and officially opened on September 4, 1903, with a speech by Mayor John Palmer and a concert by the Fredericton Brass Band; light refreshments were served afterwards at the home of a Mr. and Mrs. McKee. This was one of several open-air locations maintained by City Council for the very popular summer entertainment of musical band concerts. There were several local bands, both military and civilian, among which there was open rivalry for concert times and locations. Collections taken at these concerts, plus donations from private citizens, helped finance the expense of instruments, uniforms, music, and the conductor's salary. Other bandstands were on the Green at Parliament Square, at Phoenix Square, at Scully's Grove (east of Regent Street), and at Wilmot Park. Also visible in this photograph, at right, is the home of John Kilburn, owner of large lumbering operations in New Brunswick and Quebec.

Chapter 8

# Historic Homes and People

The residence of Bishop John Medley and his second wife, Margaret, at 97 Church Street, known as Beauregard or Bishopscote. Built in 1848 by Benjamin Wolhaupter, a businessman and high sheriff, this was the home of the Medley family from 1866 to 1905. Juliana and Alexander Ewing, who were attached to the British garrison and very active in Christ Church Cathedral, were frequent visitors at the Medley home.

## 2. The residence of Bishop John Richardson

The second Bishop's Court, 806 George Street, where Bishop John and Dora Richardson lived with their five children during the early 1900s. The bishop had been born in England and, when he and his wife needed domestic help, they placed an advertisement in a British newspaper. As a result, young Ada Driver immigrated to Fredericton. It was from Bishop's Court that she wrote a letter to England that sank with the *Empress of Ireland* on May 29, 1914, and that was retrieved and returned to her six months later. Ada Driver remained in Fredericton, and married George Wandless.

## 3. The current Bishop's Court, 791 Brunswick Street

In the late 1800s this was the home of Thomas Carleton Allen, a Loyalist descendant, registrar of the Supreme Court, and once the mayor of Fredericton. The professional tennis court on his property was often used when lawn tennis tournaments were held in the city, since the courts at Officers' Square could not accommodate all the matches. Visitors sitting on the Allens' verandah saw lightning strike Christ Church Cathedral in 1911, and telephoned the sexton and the fire department. T.C. Allen's son Charles spent his honeymoon at Bishop's Court with his bride, Alice Fortune, a survivor of the sinking of the *Titanic*. An architect visiting from Saint John in 1903 said that the Allen residence was the best-designed house in Fredericton.

## 4. The Jonathan Odell house at the corner of Brunswick and Church streets

The ell at the left in this photo of the Jonathan Odell house is believed to have included sleeping quarters for slaves. Jonathan Odell was born in Newark and graduated from the College of New Jersey. After teaching for one year, he studied medicine and served as a surgeon in the British army in the West Indies. He returned to England, where he was ordained as an Anglican priest, then moved back to New Jersey. In addition to his dual careers as clergyman and physician, Odell showed considerable talent as a poet. Writing satiric poetry on the eve of the American Revolution put him in disfavour with the rebels, and Odell and his family came to Fredericton with the Loyalists in 1784. He was appointed secretary, registrar, and clerk of the council in New Brunswick, positions that remained in the family for two generations. Odell was the grandfather of Clement C. Moore, and around 1825 a handwritten copy of Moore's 1822 poem "A Visit from St. Nicholas" was sent to the Odell home. The house is now the Anglican Deanery.

## 5. The Golden Ball Inn on Waterloo Row, just below Sunbury Street

The Golden Ball Inn was built by Abraham Vanderbeck (a Loyalist sergeant from New Jersey) and Cornelius Ackerman (a soldier and carpenter). It was later purchased by University of New Brunswick president W. Brydone Jack. British writer and artist Juliana Horatia Ewing and her soldier husband, Alexander (Rex), lived in one half of the building for almost a year (1867-1868) during his 27-month posting with the British garrison in Fredericton. They called the place *Reka Dom*, Russian for "river house."

## 6. Evelyn Grove, Lemuel Allan Wilmot's estate

Evelyn Grove, the estate of Lemuel Allan Wilmot, on the Maryland Road. The site today is at the southwest corner of Regent and Aberdeen streets. A lawyer by training, Wilmot represented York County in the House of Assembly from 1834 to 1851, when he became the first non-Anglican judge of the Supreme Court of New Brunswick. He was later the first native-born lieutenant-governor (1868-1873) of New Brunswick. He was a man of many talents beyond his legal and political careers. His interest and skill in horticulture made his estate famous. In addition to hayfields, pastures, orchards, and gardens, he also kept bees and had a greenhouse, grapery, and potting and "forcing" houses. He extended his hospitality to many people and events, including several large-scale bazaars held by the Methodist church. A seniors' complex called Evelyn Grove stands on this site today.

This picture has two images, taken from slightly different points of view; when seen through a stereoscope, it appears three dimensional. George Taylor produced numerous stereographs of a variety of scenes for what was a popular pastime in the nineteeth century.

## 8. The temporary residence of Lieutenant-Governor Sir Howard Douglas following the fire at the Governor's Mansion 1825

When lawyer Charles Putnam lived at this King Street residence, he called it Willow Grove. From the mid-1860s this was the home of John Campbell Allen, mayor of Fredericton and later chief justice of the New Brunswick Supreme Court; he was knighted in 1889. Around 1896, merchant Fred B. Edgecombe purchased the house, which he called Ashburton Place, after the birthplace of his father in England. Fred Edgecombe is at the centre of this photograph, holding a dog, with his dry goods wagon in front of his new home. Edgecombe made extensive renovations, adding turrets to extend space on the top floor and an open verandah from the front entry and along the east side of the house. The now elegant residence still stands at 736 King Street, just below St. John Street.

## 9. Linden Hall, residence of George E. Fenety, on lower Brunswick Street, with Christ Church Cathedral in the background

Well-known gardener John Bebbington was responsible for the beautiful gardens and landscaping on this lower Brunswick Street property. Born in Nova Scotia, George Fenety came to New Brunswick and established the first penny newspaper in the Maritime Provinces. He moved to Fredericton in 1863 and was the Queen's Printer until 1895. While serving as mayor, he offered his $200 annual salary towards putting a clock in the tower of the new City Hall. He was also responsible for having a double row of elm trees planted along the Green, and that section of Queen Street was known for a time as Fenety Avenue. Linden Hall was destroyed by fire in the early 1900s.

The home of photographer George T. Taylor, at 232 Northumberland Street, where he and his wife, Mary, raised their family of two sons and four daughters. Several additions had been made to this house to accommodate the large family and Taylor's photography business. Note that all the buildings in this picture are constructed of wood, and fences enclose each property. The unpaved streets would have been very muddy in wet weather. In the background at the left is the second Exhibition Building at that site.

George T. Taylor, in his later years, and family. Seated, left to right, are C.A. (Ted) Taylor, Annie, Fannie, Mary, and Nellie. Standing, left to right, are Bessie, George, and W.P. (Will) Taylor. All four daughters became teachers; later, Fannie and Nellie left the classroom and taught at home so they could manage the household when their mother's health declined. Annie was the principal at Smythe Street School for several years. Will became a lawyer and moved to Calgary, where his sister Bessie was also living. Ted served in World War One, and then worked at several jobs before building his own store in Fredericton in 1947.

## 12. The residence of Dr. G. Clowes Brown
1886

The residence of Dr. G. Clowes Brown, at the southwest corner of Westmorland and Brunswick streets, 1886. Brown was a medical officer at the Infantry School for many years and at the Hawthorne Hill school for the hearing impaired on Forest Hill for about a decade. His property was sold to allow construction of the Windsor Hall hotel and annex in the late 1890s.

## 13. "Doctors' Corner" at York and Brunswick streets c.1900

The house at left was owned by Dr. Alfred B. Atherton in 1875. After changing owners several times, it was sold to Dr. George C. VanWart, whose son Dr. Arthur VanWart also practiced there. To the right is the home and office of Dr. John Zebulon Currie, who performed the first operation at Victoria Hospital. In 1892 he sold his practice to Dr. J.W. Bridges.

## 14. Grapelawn
## 715 Brunswick Street

This vine-covered home known as Grapelawn was owned by lawyer George A. Botsford (1807-1891). The grape vines shading the verandah had grown from roots brought in the 1820s from an upriver island, and in 1887 the grapes produced about one hundred gallons of excellent wine. The house was destroyed by fire in 1892.

## 15. The main house on the Odell estate, known as Rookwood, in the west of Fredericton

The house was built as a home for William Hunter Odell (1811-1891), eldest son of William Franklin Odell and grandson of Jonathan Odell; he inherited the property in 1844. The house was originally one storey and a half, but was enlarged in the 1860s; the barns were arranged in a hollow square entered by a large covered gateway. A lawyer, W.H. Odell was appointed deputy provincial secretary, registrar, and clerk of the Executive Council. He was made a judge of the New Brunswick Court of Common Pleas in 1838, and, later, a member of the Legislative Council and, in 1865-1866, postmaster-general. He was appointed to the Senate in 1867. On February 10, 1943, not long after the city purchased the property, the house and a large attached shed burned down to the foundations, leaving two chimneys standing. The city had recently stored 7,000 ARP (air raid precautions) gas masks (those for which there was no room at City Hall or the university) in the main house, and firemen and bystanders were able to save about 5,730 of the masks.

## 16. Riverside,
## the home of John A. and Lucy Morrison

Riverside, the home of John A. and Lucy Morrison on Lincoln Road, seen from the St. John River. While her husband managed his sawmill business, Lucy Morrison transformed her interest and talent in gardening into a substantial commercial venture. The gardens were created by John Bebbington, and Mrs. Morrison proceeded to have greenhouses built. She was very much involved in the physical labour of raising healthy plants in large quantities, getting up in the early morning to be sure that the greenhouse stoves were providing proper heat during the winter months. Her efforts became the basis for a nursery business that was in friendly competition with John Bebbington.

## 17. The Anglican rectory at 734 George Street

The Georgian-style house at 734 George Street, built as an Anglican rectory in the early 1800s and once occupied by Reverend Dr. George Goodridge Roberts (who came to Fredericton in 1874 as rector of St. Anne's Parish Church) and his family. His son Sir Charles G.D. Roberts (1860-1943) was a prolific writer of both prose and poetry who, with Bliss Carman (his cousin) and Francis Sherman, won Fredericton the title "Poets' Corner of Canada." Another son, Theodore Goodridge, an accomplished author himself, etched his initials (TGR) in one of the fan windows over the front door. Grandson Athelstan (son of Charles) etched his name in one of the kitchen windows.

## 18. Farraline Place at 776 Queen Street

(formerly Camborne House)

The house was bought by Hon. John James Fraser (1829-1896) when he was appointed lieutenant-governor of New Brunswick in 1893. His widow bequeathed the house in 1921 to the Fredericton Branch of the International Order of the King's Daughters and Sons for use as a residence for senior citizens.

## 19. Frogmore Place, west of Maryland Road

## 20. The childhood home of poet Bliss Carman, at 83 Shore Street

Frogmore Place, built on an eleven-acre section of the George Sproule estate, near the bottom of the hill just west of Maryland Road (Regent Street today). This was the home of James Holbrook, schoolmaster at the Collegiate School, in the 1830s and early 1840s; he and his wife added a west wing to the house. In 1846 Judge James Carter (later chief justice) purchased the property, which was sold in 1866 to prominent Fredericton merchant and bank president Archibald D.F. Randolph. The enlarged estate had terraced flower beds, hedges, a sodded and close-mown lawn for croquet and tennis, and a variety of fruit trees; gardener J. Valentine was in charge of the landscaping. The home remained in the Randolph family into the next generation, when it was sold to Ashley Colter.

This view shows the front of the house and its gardens, intended to face onto a street that was never built. Instead, the back of the house is on Shore Street, once known as Gas Alley because of the Fredericton Gas Works on the corner. William Bliss Carman (1861-1929), a graduate of the Collegiate School and the University of New Brunswick, demonstrated skill in athletics and in writing poetry. The latter became his lifelong profession and brought him international acclaim. He wrote his early poems here, one being etched on an upstairs window pane. The family called the sprawling twelve-room house Cosey Cottage and, after the poet's parents died, his sister turned it into a college boarding house until it was sold in 1889.

## 21. Lord and Lady Ashburnham in their garden at Ashburnham Place on upper Brunswick Street c.1920

Originally two buildings, a former inn and a private home, the house at Ashburnham Place was joined at the second floor by a glassed-in conservatory. The *porte-cochère* thus formed allowed a driveway to run through to the garden.

Maria ("Rye") Anderson, born in Fredericton in 1858, had been a forerunner of the liberated woman when she took a job as a night operator for the New Brunswick Telephone Company in 1888. Captain Thomas Ashburnham, the fifth son of the fourth earl in a prominent English family, came to Canada as a 45-year-old bachelor after graduating from Cambridge and serving in the military. After evenings spent in various taverns, he would telephone Camp's Livery Stable for a horse and carriage to transport him to his hotel, Windsor Hall. He became enchanted with the friendly voice at the telephone exchange, romance blossomed, and Thomas and Maria were married in June, 1903. Ten years later, after the deaths of his four brothers, Thomas became the sixth earl and Maria became the Countess of Ashburnham.

C H A P T E R 9

# Social Life

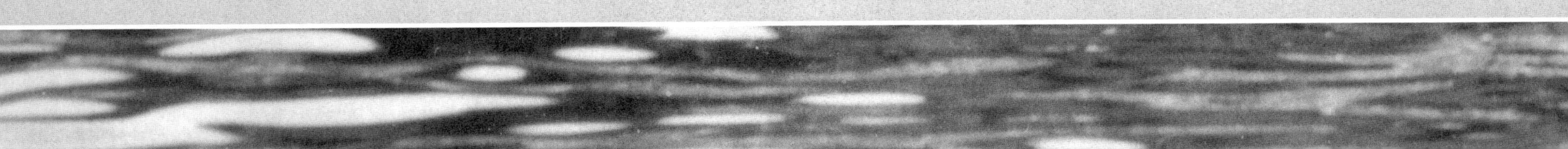

The Bicycling and Boating (B&B) Club, seen from the St. John River. In April 1895, a group of gentlemen met to form this Fredericton club, the object of which was "to promote and encourage bicycling and boating and the social advancement of its members." The club was incorporated with a capital stock of $4,000 (160 shares of $25 each), and each member had to hold at least one share. With annual dues of five dollars, the club was rather select. Members in good standing could propose names of applicants for membership and, once the managing committee had examined the eligibility of each prospective member, a vote was held at the next business meeting to accept or reject the applicant.

Construction of the clubhouse was undertaken at once, and it was officially opened on Labour Day, Monday, September 3, 1895. The clubhouse was decorated with streamers that extended to form an awning over the surrounding Green, and coloured lights added illumination. Five hundred of the 750 invitations to the evening reception were accepted, and Mayor Wesley VanWart (club president) , Lieutenant-Governor J.J. Fraser, and Dean Francis Partridge gave speeches. Refreshments of sandwiches, cake and ice cream, coffee, and ginger and lemon beer were served, and music was provided by the Citizens' Band and pianist Miss Jennie Perkins for dancing, which continued until the wee hours of the morning.

The clubhouse had boathouse facilities for about thirty canoes. The main floor had a large social room with a hardwood floor and an open fireplace, and was stocked with the best current literature. There was a code of behaviour for the clubhouse, which included prohibitions against gambling and intoxication, and members could be suspended for misconduct. The club encouraged the bicycle races between Fredericton and Springhill.

In 1913 the group changed its name to the Automobile and Boat (A & B) Club, reflecting the fact that there were then about 1,400 cars in the province. Membership was thrown open to the public, and aquatic sports were encouraged. Changing rooms for swimmers were added to the clubhouse and a float was moored in the river, which had deep water after dredging in 1912.

The Fredericton Brass Band often played at the bandstand (visible at left), adding to the enjoyment of boaters and of people walking along the Green. The dome of the Legislative Assembly building is visible in the background.

2. A bicycle tour group in front of the Bicycling and Boating Club

# 3. Tour group, with penny-farthings

A bicycle tour group, with penny-farthing bicyles, on Regent Street, circa 1886. Businesses in the background include T. McCarty at centre and the Waverley Hotel at right.

## 4. Lawn tennis at Officers' Square
c.1900

Tennis on the lawn of Officers' Square during the summer, circa 1900. Tennis was a popular and organized sport in Fredericton in the late 1800s. The Lawn Tennis Club had its meeting room in the Officers' Mess at the barracks, and tournaments were arranged. In addition to the courts at Officers' Square, the professional tennis court on the grounds of T.C. Allen at 791 Brunswick Street was sometimes also used.

"Guest Nights" or "At Homes" became fashionable during the long summer evenings. Prominent Fredericton families were invited to stroll in the Square before dinner at the Officers' Mess, a military band always playing in the background. A newspaper item from about 1901 commented on the "delightful" square, "always a model of neatness, with its spacious level lawn, huge elms and willows, and broad piazzas of the barracks."

## 5. Looking southeast across the Officers' Parade Square one hundred years ago

Ladies and gentlemen enjoy lawn tennis while a band is playing in the background. George Whelpley's Grocery Store can be seen through the trees on the other side of Queen Street. After five years as a lumber surveyor, Whelpley worked in the wholesale and retail grocery business for 40 years, with 18 to 20 of them being at this site in the Barker House block; he died in 1906. The American flag above the trees is flying from the top of a building owned by James Sharkey, a United States agent living in Fredericton at the time.

## 6. The future Wilmot Park

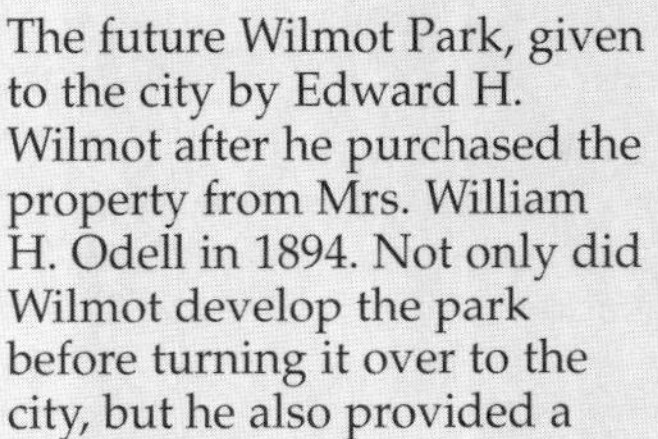

The future Wilmot Park, given to the city by Edward H. Wilmot after he purchased the property from Mrs. William H. Odell in 1894. Not only did Wilmot develop the park before turning it over to the city, but he also provided a generous financial endowment to provide for its care and further development. In this picture landscapers work near the bandstand. Across Woodstock Road are Government House and, to the left, a servant's house. The 1871 Census records indicate that at least four Government House employees (the coachman, groom, gardener, and butler) lived with their families in dwellings on the grounds of the official residence.

# 7. The Fredericton Brass Band

May 1915

Front row, left to right: J.W. Burns, H.D. McKnight, E.D. Edney, J.E. Edney, B.A. Delong, C.L. Dougherty, F.W. Thompson, C.E. Flett. Second row, left to right: F.W. Nesbett, H.B. Delong, W.J. Kelley, G.M. McCarthy, W.E. Parsons, T.E. Sutherland, F.A. Rowan, A.W. Good, R.H. Wandless, J.H. Crangle. Standing, centre: George H. Offen, Bandmaster. Third row, left to right: T. Lynch, L.B. Flett, D.W. Wallace, A.G. McFarlane, W.B. Lint, C.H. O'Connor, C.J. Toner, A.B. Baxter, B.F. Delong. Back row, left to right: R.H. O'Brien, R.C. VanWart, F.M. Kilburn, C.J. Ryan, W.J. Adams, E.P. Ryan, W.C. Burtt, R.H. Wickett.

Civilian bands had been playing in Fredericton since at least the 1840s. After a temperance organization was established in 1877, its Reform Club Band was founded. In the early 1880s it became the Fredericton Brass Band and, by the time it was the York Regiment Band sixty years later, it had become famous throughout Canada. Its first leader was J.H. Williamson, with Hugh O'Neill as assistant. The FBB, as it came to be known, played for community parades, political gatherings, various skating rinks, park picnics, and other social affairs. Programs were printed for their frequent open-air summer concerts, and many of these prized souvenirs survive. The band had outstanding singers and instrumental soloists; euphonium player Herbert G. Winter was acclaimed throughout North America. In 1908 George H. Offen, former conductor of the 71st Battalion Band, returned to Fredericton to direct the FBB, creating one of the best band sounds in Canada. Their well-publicized open-air concerts, from May 1 to September 30 each year, included new marches, popular waltzes, and novelty tunes. Between 1910 and 1915, the City Council increased its annual grant to the FBB from $150 to $500, an indication of the band's popularity. When Ernest Beatty became bandmaster, their success continued.

# 8. The Fredericton Fire Department

The first picture of the Fredericton Fire Department in full-dress uniform, taken on the stage of the Opera House in City Hall, 1899. The grand opening of the Opera House had taken place on November 8, 1876, after much careful planning. The song, "We Greet You, Loyal Citizens," was composed for the event by Professor Cadwallader of the Provincial Normal School. Oscar Wilde, the Egleston English Opera Company, and the New York Windsor Theatre Company were among those who performed on the 27- by 22-foot stage. By the time this photograph was taken, the stage had been made wider and deeper, new dressing rooms had been built, four new drop curtains had been purchased, and the building had been wired for electricity. The Opera House was able to attract John Philip Sousa and his 46-member band, Mohawk poet Pauline Johnson, violinist Mary Hall from England, and more theatre companies. It was also used to show moving pictures, before being closed during World War Two.

## 9. The St. Dunstan's Dramatic Society, in *The Bohemians* at the Opera House

April 17, 1909

Front row: A.J. Hanlon, Miss E. Purdy. Second row, left to right: Dorothy Dever, James Collins, W.A. Walsh, Miss C. Ryan, G. O'Brien. Third row, left to right: Harry Cox, L.L. Theriault, J. Walsh, Miss Mamie Roberts, J. Ryan, Greg Feeney, Ed Hanlon. Back row, left to right: Miss L. McDonald, A. O'Brien, Miss K. McClusky, P. Foster, Miss M. Foster, Johnny Dolan, Miss M. Dryden, M. Howley, Miss E. O'Brien.

This comedy-drama, under the auspices of the Young Men's Society of St. Dunstan's Church, was presented at the City Hall Opera House, which was packed to the door. The Provincial Legislature provided complimentary tickets for UNB and Normal School students, who filled the gallery. The three-act show was performed flawlessly, making it one of the best amateur productions ever given in the city. The versatile and clever impersonations of the actors "brought down the house," and brought lengthy and positive reviews in the Fredericton and Saint John press.

## 10. The cast of *The Meddlesome Maid* taking a final curtain call

St. Dunstan's Hall, March 19, 1936

From left to right are Matthew Dobbelsteyn, Helen Grannan, Walter Myshrall, Margaret Hughes, Edward Quinn, Mary Grannan, Gregory Rowan, Mary Foster, Joseph Dobbelsteyn, Dorothy Hughes, and Edward Carten. The little girl in front is May Savage. Mary Grannan, an elementary-school teacher, went on to have her own weekly radio show on the local station, CFNB, and then nation-wide children's radio and television series on the CBC. In addition, she wrote thirty top-selling children's books, many of them published simultaneously in Canada, the United States, and Great Britain.

## 11. The cast of a University of New Brunswick Drama Society production

c.1931

Seated, left to right: Don Jamer, Irene Harrison, Professor R.E.D. Cattley, Margaret Smith, Carl Watson. Standing, left to right: Horace Hanson, Marjorie McMurray, Mavis Downey.

## 12. The Gem Theatre at the southeast corner of King and Carleton streets

Established in a renovated tenement building in May 1910 by David M. Richards, the Gem Theatre had a local orchestra to accompany the silent-screen movies it showed. Fred G. Spencer of Saint John leased the Gem in 1917 and made extensive renovations to create a modern theatre with a seating capacity of 451. After a disastrous fire in December 1919, Spencer built a much larger theatre, the Capitol, on the same site; it opened in 1922. Eight years later it was purchased by Witter Fenety and remained in business until 1973.

Fredericton has a long history of motion picture theatres, beginning in 1907 with the Wonderland and the Nickel, and continuing with the Palace, the Carleton, and the Bijou. William Fenety opened the Unique motion picture theatre in the Masonic Hall on Carleton Street in 1908 and, with his son Witter, opened the Gaiety Theatre on the ground floor of the nearby Anglican church hall in 1913. The Unique and the Gaiety amalgamated in 1917 and reopened as the New Gaiety in a newly constructed building on Queen Street. Following a disastrous fire in 1939, the third Gaiety continued in business in a new 900-seat theatre on the same Queen Street site.

## 13. A SLEIGH RIDE ON THE ST. JOHN RIVER
1885

Besides sleigh rides, the river was a popular location for tobogganing and skating. On December 1, 1884, over one thousand people were skating on the river between Sherman's Wharf (on the south bank near the Cathedral) and Gibson's Tannery (on the north bank). In the background are Christ Church Cathedral on the left, the Legislative Assembly in the centre, with the office and warehouse of lumber merchant D.F. George on the shore in front, and several Queen Street buildings on the right.

## 14. Five men from the 22nd Regiment on a toboggan
1867

From left to right are a Mr. Newington, Lieutenant Backhouse, Ensign Natherson, Lieutenant Parry, and Lieutenant Collins. The sport was possibly introduced to Fredericton by the British garrison. In 1886 Mr. John Edwards, manager of the Queen Hotel, built a first-class toboggan slide in front of the Legislative Assembly. It was 148 feet long and its incline was sufficient to send sliders far out onto the frozen river. The slide was so popular that Edwards built a more elaborate one the next year. The sport spread to Government House and, in January, 1888, Lady Tilley issued "Tobogganing At Home Cards" for several Saturday afternoons that winter.

## 15. The Fredericton Snowshoe Club on an outing in the woods

From left to right are Ernest Crewdson, David Crowe, William T. Chestnut (of R. Chestnut & Sons Ltd.), an unidentified man, and Harry G. Chestnut. The club was formed in December 1884, largely by members of the Lawn Tennis Club. Gentlemen wishing to join had to submit their names to the secretary, and lady members were nominated by the gentlemen members. The club chose as its uniform "a blue blanket coat with scarlet sash and a blue tuque." Snowshoe tramps and the election of additional members were done on a weekly basis. Although snowshoes were a necessary part of life for many, they also became a recreational activity, and by the late 1800s, snowshoeing parties had become a popular part of the city's social life.

## 16. The circular Fredericton Skating Rink, interior view

The Fredericton Skating Club was incorporated in 1864 and, in September 1868, a site at the southwest corner of York and Saunders streets was chosen for a first-class skating rink. Built on the design of the Victoria Rink in Saint John, the huge polygon-shaped rink opened amid fanfare on December 17, 1868. There were crowds on the ice and groups of spectators all around the circular platform at ground level. From the central balcony above, the band of the 22nd Regiment played. Soldiers of the Imperial regiments were the most enthusiastic supporters, so attendance declined after the troops left in May 1869. The building was not maintained, and in 1880 skating was cancelled. On April 9, 1881, the rink was destroyed in a spectacular blaze of uncertain origin.

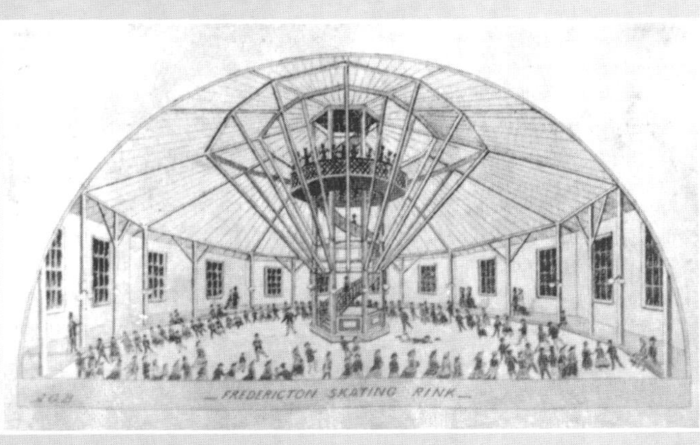


## 17. The Arctic Rink, built in 1902 on Carleton Street near the highway bridge

Shaped like a Quonset hut behind its brick facade, The Arctic Rink was the largest rink in the Maritimes at that time. Inside, there was a promenade platform at ground level, as well as a balcony around the rink and space for a band on the upper level. Some 1,200 citizens of all ages came for the grand opening on December 25, 1902. The rink provided a venue for public skating, hockey games, figure skating, and speedskating in winter, and sometimes roller skating, bowling, and political and religious meetings in the off-seasons. On April 30, 1939, Fredericton lost its second indoor skating rink in a disastrous fire.

## 18. The Boys of Summer baseball teams
1902

Front row, left to right: Harry F. McLeod, William "Doc" Kelly, Dr. Frederick J. Seery, Fred B. Edgecombe, C. Fred Chestnut, Thomas Carleton Allen, Fred S. Hilyard, Dr. James Bridges, T. Bradshaw Winslow, A.F. Street, James H. Hawthorne, Matthew Tennant. Second row, left to right: James T. Sharkey, Dr. George J. McNally, Dr. William C. Crocket, John Palmer, R.W.L. Tibbits, James H. Crocket, Albert Edgecombe, Dr. Fred Gunter, Robert P. Foster, George Y. Dibblee, Loran C. MacNutt. Back row, left to right: D. Lee Babbitt, John Kilburn, F. St. John Bliss.

During the 1880s, baseball became a popular sport, and the Fredericton Baseball Club was formed in 1886. The numerous teams played their games at Scully's Grove, an open area east of Regent Street, where the owner of the land, William Scully, had the dugouts and bleachers installed. When the doctors and trustees of the Victoria Public Hospital showed a desire to have an X-ray machine, a very recent invention, the $500 cost presented an obstacle. A baseball challenge was proposed as a fundraiser, and elaborate plans were made to form a Hospital Nine and a Citizens' Nine, complete with distinctive uniforms and rules. When Dominion Day was rained out, the game was rescheduled for July 8; since it was a Tuesday, all stores, factories, mills, and schools were closed early so everyone could arrive for the four o'clock game. Twelve hundred citizens turned out to see the Hospital Nine win the game 26 to 25, and $300 was raised from admission fees and sale of refreshments. With the gift of $200 from gentleman farmer Charles H. Giles of Kingsclear, the hospital was able to purchase the X-ray machine.

CHAPTER 10

# TRANSPORTATION AND VISITORS

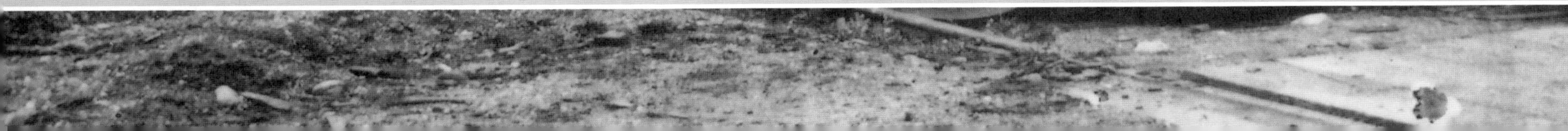

1. *Illustrated London News*
THE ARRIVAL OF THE PRINCE OF WALES
1860

The arrival of Queen Victoria's eldest son, Prince Albert Edward, Prince of Wales, at Fredericton on August 4, 1860, as drawn by artist G.H. Andrews. The 18-year-old prince made a lengthy and successful tour of the British North American colonies and parts of the United States. The tour received extensive and detailed coverage on both sides of the Atlantic. He travelled from the Kennebecasis to Fredericton and back to Saint John on the freshly painted paddle-wheeler *Forest Queen*. In the capital city, he inspected a volunteer guard of honour, attended divine service at Christ Church Cathedral (where he presented an inscribed Bible, still in existence), officially opened what later became Wilmot Park, and attended a gala ball. A guest at Government House during his visit in Fredericton, he also took an impromptu trip by canoe across the St. John River and back with Maliseet guide Gabe Atwin.

## 2. Paddle-wheel steamers at the Star Line Pier

Paddle-wheel steamers moored at the Star Line Pier at the river bank in front of Officers' Square and the foot of Regent Street, in 1899. From left to right are the *David Weston* (built in 1866 and burned in 1903), the *Victoria* (built in 1897 and broken up in 1916), and the *Aberdeen* (built in 1894 and broken up in 1908). The steamers were both an important transportation link for commerce and a pleasant means of recreation. In the background are the Lemont building, the dome of the Legislative Building, and the spire of Christ Church Cathedral.

## 3. The staff in the dining saloon of the paddle-wheel steamer *Victoria* 1902

In an age when a trans-Atlantic crossing might take two weeks, a journey from Saint John to Fredericton would require several hours. Thus, good dining facilities for passengers was important.

## 4. A handbill advertising the Star Line S.S. Company

# STAR LINE S. S. COMPANY.

## River Saint John.

## SAINT JOHN AND FREDERICTON.

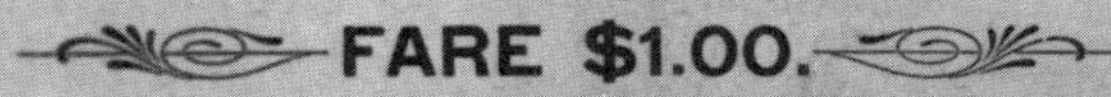

## FARE $1.00.

## SUMMER ARRANGEMENT.

EASTERN STANDARD TIME.

One of the splendid new MAIL STEAMERS, "**Victoria**" and "**David Weston,**" will leave St. John, North End, for Fredericton and intermediate landings, every morning, Sunday excepted, at 8.00 o'clock, and will leave Fredericton for St. John and intermediate landings every morning, Sundays excepted, at 8.00 o'clock, due at St. John at 1.30 p. m.

Connections with trains of the Canadian Pacific Railway for Woodstock, Aroostook, Grand Falls, Edmundston, etc.; with Canada Eastern Railway for Doaktown, Chatham, etc. Connection made with Electric Cars of St. John City Railway, which run to and from Steamboat Landing.

**Excursion Tickets** from St. John to Fredericton and intermediate points, also from Fredericton to St. John, etc., issued on Saturday at **One Fare**, good to return free on Monday following, but no return ticket less than forty cents.

**SPECIAL EXCURSION RATES.**—For the benefit of visitors and tourists who wish to make a trip on the St. John River to Fredericton and return the same day, a special arrangement has been made by the Canadian Pacific Railway Company and the Star Line Steamers, whereby a Round Trip Ticket will be issued during the Summer months for the fare of $2.00, enabling passengers to go to Fredericton by boat every day, leaving Fredericton same night, or on any train following day. Saturday tickets good to return on following Monday.

FREDERICTON TO WOODSTOCK.—While water is high, Steamer "**Aberdeen**" will leave Fredericton every Tuesday, Thursday and Saturday, at 5.30 a. m., and returning, leave Woodstock on alternate days at 6.30 a. m., due at Fredericton at 1.00 p. m.

BELLEISLE ROUTE.—Steamer "**Springfield**" leaves Indiantown every Tuesday, Thursday and Saturday at 11 24 a. m., for Springfield, Kings Co., returning alternate days, arriving at 1.00 p. m.

On and after June 17th Steamer "**Aberdeen**" will leave her wharf at Indiantown every Saturday at 5.30 p. m., for Wickham and intermediate landings; returning will leave Wickham every Monday morning, arriving in St. John about 8.30.

**Improved Accommodation. First-Class Tables. Fast Scheduled Time will be Guaranteed.**

HEAD OFFICE AT STAR LINE WHARF, INDIANTOWN, ST. JOHN, N. B.

JAMES MANCHESTER, PRESIDENT.

R. S. ORCHARD. SEC.-TREAS.

The services of local photographers were used to promote tourism and travel. In 1902 it was reported that H.F. Albright had been in Saint John to do business with the E.F. Skillings Company for about 300 photographs for upcoming steamboat art albums. George Taylor and George Schleyer also advertised their scenic views of the city and other locations in New Brunswick.

## 5. Fredericton's first highway bridge, built of wood in 1885

On November 27, 1885, citizens turned out en masse to attend the opening of their first bridge across the St. John River. The structure was three times larger than any other bridge built until then in New Brunswick. The eleven spans, including the turntable draw, plus the approaches, measured about 3,000 feet. The swing draw span gave two 60-foot openings for navigation purposes. The piers, filled with well-packed ballast (rocks hauled in by local farmers), were built of cedar rather than stone, and rested under water on a cribwork of hardwood and hemlock timbers, with tamarack piles driven into the river bed. The bridge was partly destroyed by fire in August 1905, and was replaced by a steel bridge, with the two burned spans being replaced first. Chief Bridge Engineer Rainsford Wetmore insisted on building the new structure several feet higher than the wooden bridge; this probably saved the newer highway bridge during the 1936 flood.

## 6. A stereograph looking through Fredericton's first highway bridge

This stereographic image gives a good idea of the trestle work and bracing involved in the construction of a wooden bridge. The roadway was 24 feet wide overall. The walkway (added later as a result of a letter-writing campaign to the local press) was five feet wide on the upriver side. The flooring was four-inch spruce planks which, like the rest of the bridge materials, had to be free from sap, shakes, wanes, rotten knots, and any other defects.The man in the photo is George Miles, the first caretaker.

## 7. An early locomotive engine with its "flanger"

An early locomotive engine, photographed at the old Fredericton race course, west of the CPR station on York Street, in the early 1870s. The two pieces of boiler plate attached to the lower part of the engine's "cowcatcher" were raised and lowered from inside the cab to scrape away snow and slush from the rail tops and the space inside the rails. Credit for first inventing this railway "flanger" has been given to John Hamilton, a blacksmith who worked at the Devon roundhouse for the old New Brunswick Railway Company. However, Henry Miller, an engineer on the Fredericton Branch Railway, may, in fact, have been the first: *The Reporter* announced that a model of Miller's patented "Ice and Snow Flanger for locomotives" would be on display at the Fredericton Exhibition in October 1873. Standing beside the engine are Alexander "Boss" Gibson (left), lumberman and owner of the large cotton mill in Marysville, and Fred B. Edgecombe, a railway agent who sold tickets for many years at his dry goods store on Queen Street. Exhibition Palace is in the background.

## 8. An arch prepared for the visit of Sir John A. and Lady Macdonald

August 1887

This magnificent evergreen arch was constructed across lower Queen Street near the offices of *The Capital* newspaper; the inscription on the upper side was "Welcome to Sir John and Lady." Canada's first prime minister was accompanied by his second wife, Agnes, on this significant non-political visit to Fredericton. She had pleasant memories of a former visit to the city and encouraged Sir John to come on this occasion. Thousands of spectators from all over the province lined the streets of Fredericton to see the 73-year-old politician. Businesses in the background include G.T. Whelpley's Grocery Store and S.F. Shute Watches and Jewelry. Another arch spanned York Street near the Edgecombe Building.

9. A large crowd watching Lady Macdonald as she lays the cornerstone of Fredericton's first railway bridge
August 15, 1887

Three New Brunswick newspapers, some coins, and a memo about the stone laying were placed in a tin box that Lady Macdonald in turn placed in a cavity in the cornerstone of the railway bridge. The stone was sealed over with mortar, then lowered into place. Standing beside the cornerstone, from left to right, are Lieutenant-Governor Samuel Leonard Tilley, Lady Macdonald, Senator Thomas Temple, Sub-Dean Finlow Alexander of Christ Church Cathedral, and Gilmore Brown, designer of the bridge. The gentleman seated above the excavation with his hand on his cane is Sir John A. Macdonald; Lady Tilley is seated on his right. The day following this ceremony, Lady Macdonald held a reception at Government House.

## 10. The first train crossing Fredericton's new railway bridge 1888

The first train to cross the bridge consisted of one locomotive and four flatcars, the last carrying a group of workers. The bridge, built by the Dominion Bridge Co.Ltd. of Lachine, Quebec, had been under construction for almost a year. It had nine spans resting on granite piers, with level crossings at each end. At the official opening on June 20, 1888, a large crowd gathered to watch a train with two cars of passengers pass over the bridge and back. On March 19, 1936, the crushing surge of ice during a record-breaking freshet lifted the spans from the piers and deposited them on the river bed, leaving twisted rails on the shore.

## 11. The first passenger train passing over Fredericton's second railway bridge

June 1, 1938

The second railway bridge was built to replace the structure destroyed in 1936. When the new bridge was built, it was made six feet higher, and an underpass was constructed at each end to replace the former level crossings.

## 12. The Vice-Regal party and the reception committee at the York Street (Union) Railway Station

July 22, 1935

Left to right: Major T.C. Barker, Official Secretary to the Lieutenant Governor; Captain M.E. Adeane, ADC to the Governor General; Lieutenant-Governor Murray MacLaren; Governor-General Bessborough; Lady Bessborough; Premier A.A. Dysart; Hon. R.B. Hanson, Federal Minister of Trade and Commerce; Captain D. Fisher-Rowe, ADC to the Governor General; Hon. Dr. W.F. Roberts, Provincial Minister of Health and Labour; Hon. A.P. Paterson, President of the New Brunswick Executive Council; Lord Duncannon, son of Their Excellencies; Colonel E.D. MacKenzie, Comptroller at Rideau Hall; Major C.M. Scott, ADC to the Lieutenant Governor. Governor-General Bessborough and his family chose Fredericton as the place to begin their final official tour of Canada.

## 13. Railway officials and the reception committee at Union Station

August 9, 1935

Left to right, in the front row: Fredericton Mayor W.G. Clark, CPR President Sir Edward Beatty (hand in pocket), New Brunswick Premier A.A. Dysart, Bank of Montreal President Sir Charles Gordon, Steel Company of Canada President Ross McMaster, Royal Bank of Canada President M.W. Wilson, and Senator Smeaton White.

The first railway station on this site was a two-storey wooden structure with waiting rooms on the ground level and offices on the second floor. It was ready for occupancy in the fall of 1869, and on December 1, the first regular passenger train on the newly built Fredericton Branch Line to Hartt's Mills (later Fredericton Junction) departed. On that initial excursion of 22 miles, which took just over one hour, there were many distinguished guests, including Lieutenant-Governor Lemuel Allan Wilmot, Judge Charles Fisher, Sheriff Thomas Temple, Alexander "Boss" Gibson, Mayor George Gregory, former mayor William Needham, the city aldermen, clergymen, several senators, and members of Parliament and the Legislature.

The initial complaint that the railway station was too far out of town (there was little settlement beyond Charlotte Street in 1869) was forgotten by the 1920s, when the city had grown and rail traffic was thriving. A new brick station, 28 feet wide and 150 feet long (including 24-foot canopies at the east and west ends) received its first travellers on December 22, 1923. The first formal inspection took place on January 3, 1924, with CPR Vice-President A.D. McTier meeting with Premier P.J. Veniot. Various features of the Union Station (serving both CPR and CNR lines) can be seen in this picture: the ornamental base border of sandstone, the cupola design for the second floor that provided office space, the decorative red tile cross in the canopy gable, and part of the octagonal office (at right) for the station master, ticket agent, and telegraph operator. Inside were two waiting rooms, one for the general public and one for women only, with oak seats, doors, and ceiling beams. There were hardwood floors throughout.

The old wooden station was moved to the corner of Victoria and Northumberland streets, where it still stands.

## 14. The Intercolonial Railway (ICR) Station on Brunswick Street

Photographed May 15, 1903 by Rocke & Davidson of Saint John

The completion of the railway bridge in 1888 allowed extended service to Fredericton by the New Brunswick Railway (from Rivière du Loup) and the Northern & Western Railway (from Chatham and Newcastle). The connection of these two systems at Gibson was completed on June 14, and the first train crossed the new bridge on June 15, 1888. The Northern & Western offices were removed from the north side of the river, and the Bridge Company erected a "temporary" station on the south side, on Brunswick Street. Beginning on October 1, N & W trains arrived at and departed from the Fredericton Station instead of at Gibson, and all freight was received and delivered at this new facility. The station, pictured here, remained in use for more than two decades.

In 1910, the Board of Trade criticized the poor condition of the ICR station, and pointed out that the federal government had allocated money in 1908 for a new station in Fredericton. Government and railway officials visited the city in September 1910, and plans began for the construction of a new brick station and the repositioning of some sections of railway track. In late August 1911, the old station's baggage room was removed, and construction of a temporary freight house was begun. Excavation started for the new ICR station, to be located just behind the old one, which allowed for use of the existing station office and waiting rooms during the building process. Work was delayed by a scarcity of bricklayers and masons, but the project was completed by the spring of 1912. A wide, concrete platform was built from Brunswick to George streets. (The ICR station later became the CNR station, and was demolished in the late 1960s.)

The first station was moved and used as a temporary freight shed until a new freight storage building was constructed in 1913-1914 on four acres of land expropriated from the Timothy Lynch property (formerly Evelyn Grove). In 1914, City Council approved the new ICR route through Fredericton, a plan that allowed the new tracks to pass close to both the ICR and CPR freight-handling facilities.

## 15. Four Fredericton-area residents who left for the Yukon Gold Rush

March 1, 1898

From left to right are George Pinder, R.D.W. Hubbard, George Black, and George Amireaux. Messrs. Pinder, Black, and Amireaux were members of The Fredericton Mining and Development Company, backed by a syndicate of New Brunswick businessman and politicians. They, along with William Boddy, George Graham, Samuel Hoskins, and Humphrey Boone, were among the 24 young men who left in a special coach attached to the Montreal Express. One thousand citizens gathered at the CPR train station on York Street to bid farewell to this first major Yukon-bound exodus from the city. Travelling across Canada by train and then by steamer and snowshoe, they met other Frederictonians, including Harry Waugh and Walter Chestnut (the latter dying in the North) once they reached the heart of the Yukon. George Black wrote long letters home and to the editor of *The Daily Gleaner*; the letters to the newspaper were published and provided splendid accounts of his experiences. He also sent photographs, pressed flowers, dried skins of small animals, and the occasional gold nugget. He remained in the North, becoming Member of Parliament in Ottawa for the Yukon Territory; his wife, Martha, took his place in the House of Commons when he was ill, and she thus became the second woman ever elected to Parliament.

Chapter 11

# Hotels

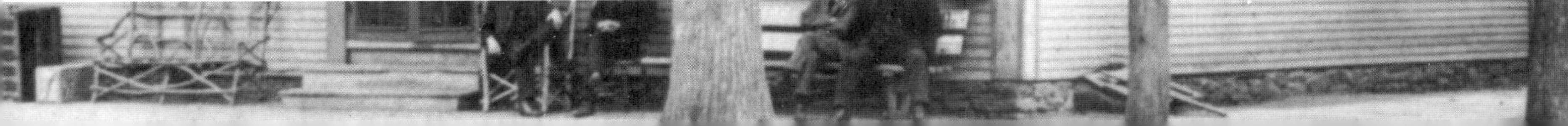

The original Barker House Hotel on Queen Street, before it was expanded, with the Barker Alley on the right. When proprietor Spafford Barker opened his new brick hotel on May 18, 1853, he chose high-quality black walnut and mahogany furnishings and had up-to-date plumbing in the four-storey structure. After Fred B. Coleman purchased the hotel circa 1888, *The Capital* announced that he wished to run a livery stable in connection with the Barker House and had therefore leased the nearby Spahnn property occupied by the Albion Hotel. Mr. Coleman also put on display in the Barker House lobby a huge stuffed frog, supposedly from Killarney Lake near Fredericton; the frog was later moved to the York-Sunbury Museum. In 1907, ownership of the Barker House passed to T.V. Monahan, who expanded the hotel to 75 rooms when he leased and renovated the former Royal Hotel. This Barker House Annex had 28 rooms, including ten rooms that were two-room suites with private bathrooms.

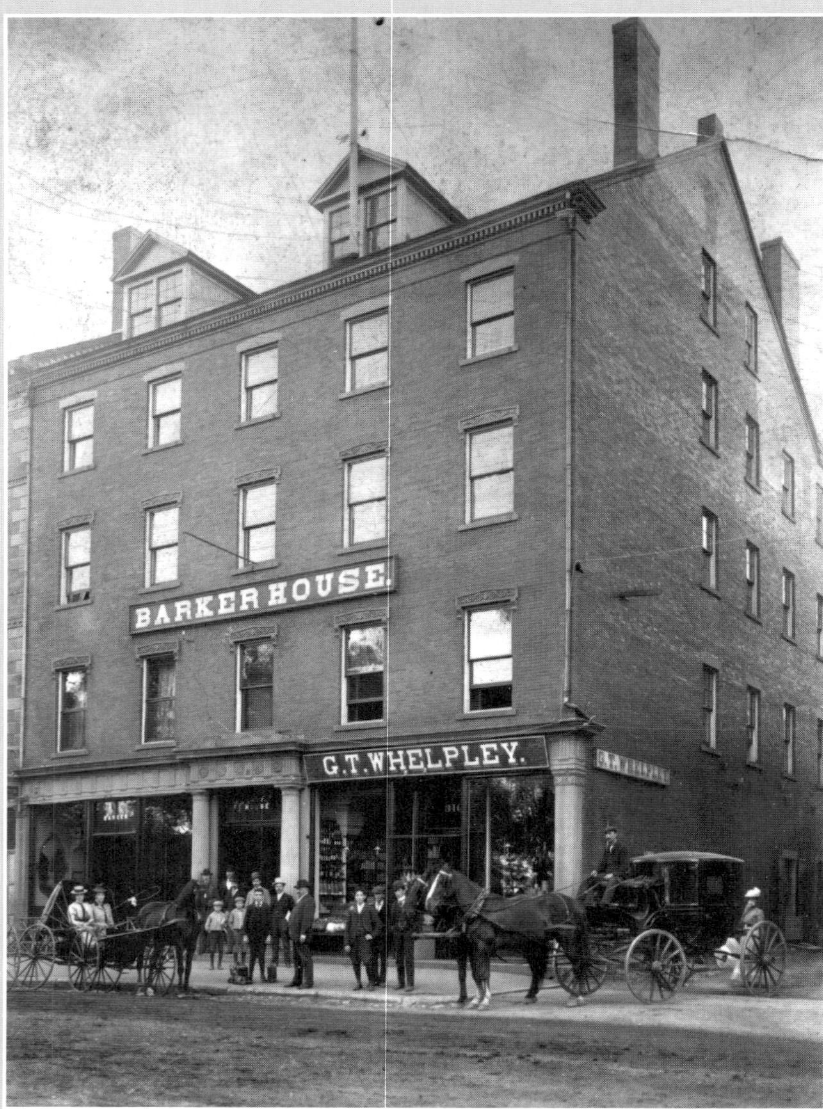

## 2. The South Side of Lower Queen Street, Looking West toward Regent Street

The Queen Hotel stands out in this photograph. The Queen and the Barker House were the two most prominent hotels in Fredericton during the last three decades of the 1800s, being joined in 1897 by a strong new competitor—Windsor Hall.

The Queen Hotel, built by the Fredericton Hotel Company, opened in 1869 with William Wheeler as the owner. A circular stairwell led from the rotunda-like foyer to three storeys above, 60 large bedrooms (with various family suites), and a bridal chamber. Wheeler hired an energetic and sociable desk clerk, 24-year-old J.A. (Jack) Edwards, who became the manager in 1881. After buying the hotel, Edwards made extensive interior renovations, updating the plumbing, adding a barber shop and a billiard room, placing a piano and mahogany furniture in the ladies' parlour, and expanding the elegant dining room to seat 100.

When Edwards became postmaster in 1902, John J. McCaffrey purchased the Queen. Management passed to Terence V. Monahan in 1922 and to J.P. Corkery in 1933, before the building was put into use as government offices in 1948.

## 3. The dining room of the Queen Hotel
c.1930

The dining room of the Queen Hotel, circa 1930. Standing in the background are Mayor W.G. Clark and City Clerk Fred Haviland. Local artists had been hired in 1887 to decorate the walls in high relief, and the ceilings were panelled and rosetted with gilt mouldings. The tables were set with imported linen, costly silver and china, and high-quality crystal. Electricity replaced the original gas lighting, and the elegant dining room was the scene of elaborate dinners and government receptions, as well as fine dining for the general public.

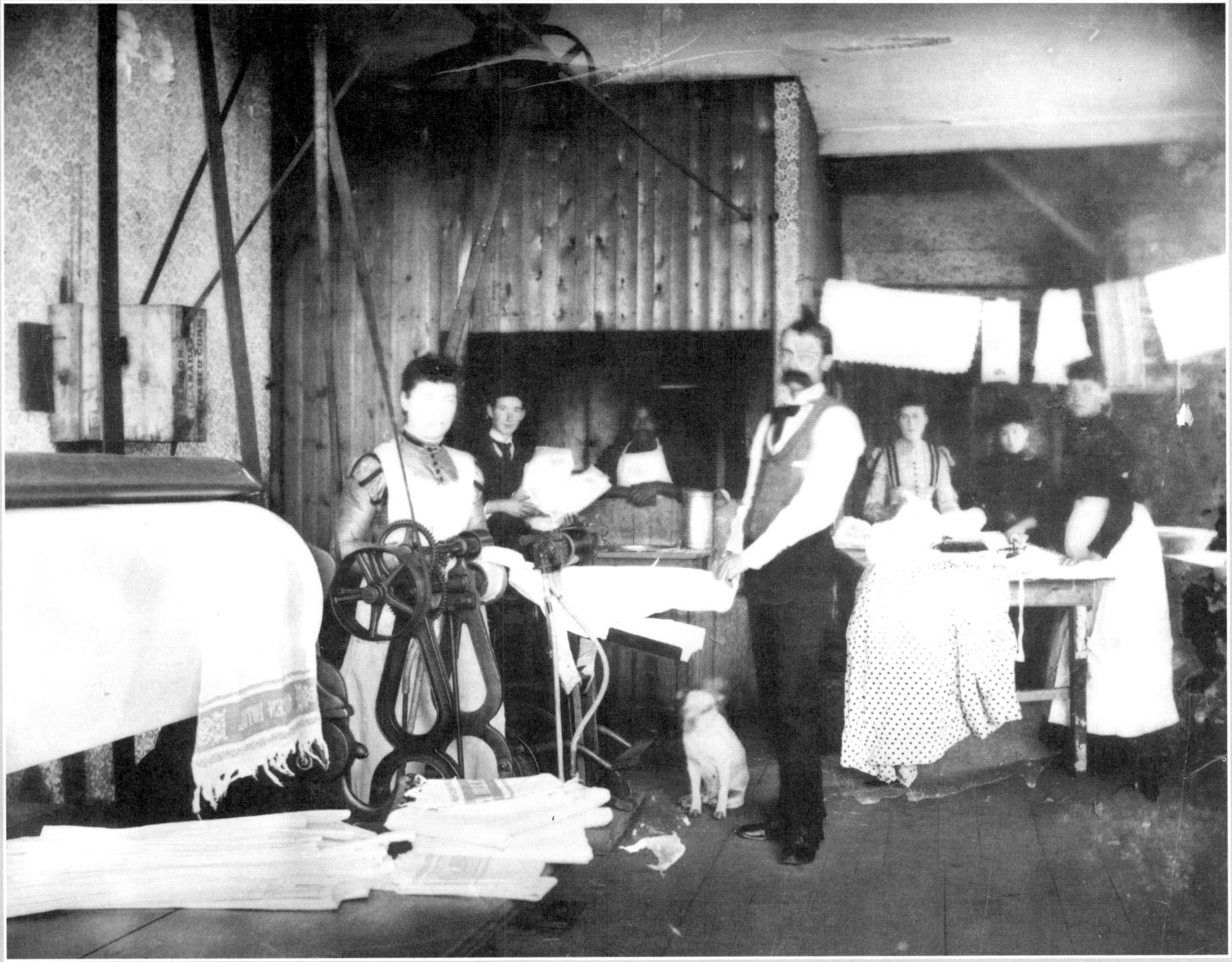

The towel coming through the wringer bears the Queen Hotel monogram. This may be the Globe Laundry, which operated for many years just down the street from the hotel, or the laundry built at the Queen Hotel in 1885.

John B. Grieves Stabling (left), the Waverley Hotel (centre), and the Lorne Hotel (right) on Regent Street. Built in 1851 by William Grieves, the Waverley was later operated by his son John. The four-storey main block had a three-storey addition at the back. In December 1886, not long after a new furnace had been installed, a fire started at the foot of the main stairway of the Waverley and caused extensive damage to both hotels, as well as to the Grieves Grocery Store. Repairs were made to the Waverley House, and it continued in business into the 1930s, when H.E. Dewar & Son were the proprietors. The Lorne Hotel continued in business, with Feeney & Jamieson advertised as owners in 1917; in 1919 Harold M. Young operated Young's Lorne Hotel.

# 6. Windsor Hall

# 7. Windsor Hall and the Windsor Annex

Windsor Hall, at the southwest corner of Brunswick and Westmorland streets, formerly the Clowes Brown property. The four-storey wooden structure was built in 1897 for owners Mr. and Mrs. Albert Everett. The up-to-date hotel, with its fifty incandescent electric lights, appealed to the public, and a three-storey annex built out of concrete blocks was added along the Westmorland Street side in 1899. The annex contained apartment-style units for long-term guests, some of them permanent city residents. The dining room had a reputation for generous servings of plain, wholesome food, and the hotel was popular with farmers who came to town the day before market day. When the Earl of Ashburnham first came to Fredericton, he stayed at the Windsor until his marriage to Maria Anderson. Ownership of the hotel passed from the Everetts to the Thurrott family. Eventually the hotel was renovated for other uses, and it was destroyed by fire in 1983.

## 8. The York Hotel, at the southeast corner of King and Westmorland streets

The second or third hotel of this name, it is believed by some to have been the home of Charles Fisher, son of Peter Fisher, considered the first historian of New Brunswick. Charles Fisher represented York County in the Legislative Assembly almost continuously from 1837 to 1868, served for a time as premier and attorney general, and was a delegate to the Quebec and London conferences that led to Confederation. He was made a puisne judge of the province's Supreme Court in 1868. The Fisher home was later converted into apartments and, finally, into a hotel.

Numerous other hotels came and went during the 1800s in Fredericton; others changed their names or locations. McLeod's Inn at the head of Waterloo Row became the Waterloo Coffee House in 1818. The Golden Ball Inn, after two name changes, relocated as the Golden Ball to another site on Waterloo Row in the 1830s or 1840s. Auliff's Hotel near the steamboat wharf at Regent Street became Jackson's Hotel in the 1830s and another York Hotel in 1856. Mr. Atherton enlarged his City Hotel to forty beds in 1863 by adding a third storey and an extension at the rear; his livery stables added "a silver coach and several light pleasure waggons" at the same time, according to *The Reporter*. In the 1880s the Royal Hotel, Magee House, the Albion Hotel, the Exchange Hotel, and the Carvell Hotel were all operating along Queen Street. King Street had Long's Hotel and Mooer's Hotel, and there was the Victoria on Regent Street.

C H A P T E R 12

# FLOODS

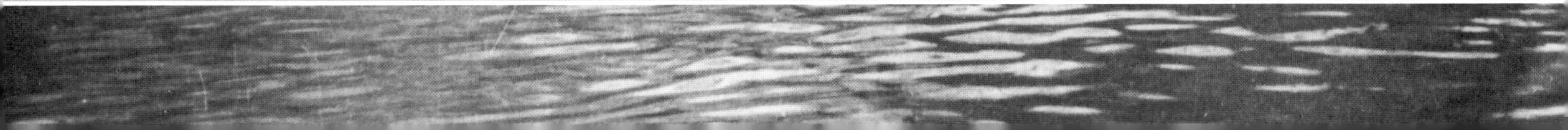

## 1. Brunswick and York streets, looking east, during the flood of 1863

This low-lying section of Brunswick Street, just north of the small hill on which the Old Burying Ground is located, continues to be prone to flooding when the St. John River is in freshet. The fence on the right runs along the cemetery.

2. Waterloo Row during the flood of 1887, with a steamer and wood boat tied up at the roadside

## 3. Officers' Square during the 1887 freshet

A submerged Officers' Square during the freshet of May 1887. The soldiers in the canoe were members of the Infantry School Corps. Dugald Campbell, the engineer who laid out the early streets of Fredericton, commented in 1807 on how low and flat the land was and how quickly the Barrack Yard could become "a pond of water or a bed of deep mud" with the least rain.

## 4. Floodwaters near the Gas Works
1887

Flooded streets during the spring freshet of 1887. The smokestack and low buildings of the Gas Works (at Shore Street and University Avenue) are visible in the background at right. From about 1847 to the 1890s, Fredericton street lamps, fuelled by coal gas produced at this plant, illuminated the thoroughfares with a yellowish glow. The Gas Light Company acquired competition in the 1880s, when a power station was built on Carleton Street. In May 1888, both companies submitted tenders to provide illumination for 28 street lights. *The Capital* reported that the installation of incandescent electric lights at Morrison's Mill had been completed by the end of November 1888, although there was the occasional injury as workers adjusted to the new technology.

By 1901 a new "Brush arc lamp dynamo" had been purchased from the Canadian General Electric Company in Toronto to improve street light service, the new lamps providing a steady, bluish light. By 1902 the Fredericton Electric Light Company had built another coal shed and added a 250 hp water heater to improve the plant and provide all-night service. Since all-day service was not available, many people had to install pipes for acetylene as well.

By December 1910, the Fredericton Gas Light Company began 24-hour electric service and advertised that they would wire houses at cost. For a monthly fee of $1.25, a customer could burn four 20-candle-power tungsten lights at one time, "night and day if necessary."

## 5. The wooden highway bridge
1887

The Fredericton highway bridge, seen from the north side during the 1887 freshet. The wooden bridge received very little damage from the ice, but the ice pile seen here did not totally melt until June. It was fire, and not floods or ice jams, that eventually destroyed the bridge.

## 6. The ice jam behind City Hall
c.1902

## 7. Lower Queen Street, during the 1936 flood

A flood scene on lower Queen Street, showing floodwaters and ice around the Temple fountain, the Automobile and Boat Club, the Burns Monument, and the east-end bandstand, on March 20, 1936. Thomas Temple was High Sheriff for twenty years and was one of the principal organizers of The People's Bank, founded in 1864. Involved in building railways, he was a partner in the Fredericton Bridge Company. He represented York-Sunbury in the House of Commons from 1884 until 1896, when he was appointed to the Senate. He presented Fredericton with a watering trough surmounted by a reclining metal lion with a large basin for horses, a small basin for dogs and cats, and drinking facilities on the sides, with metal cups attached, for people. The two old muzzle-loading cannons (in the background) were leftovers from the Imperial regiments of the 1880s and were given to the city by Jabez Bunting Snowball during his term as lieutenant-governor (1902-1907). In 1942 they were donated to the federal government to be made over into modern implements of war.

## 8. St. John Street in flood

1936

St. John Street in flood, March 20, 1936, the morning after an ice jam and floodwaters had lifted the first railway bridge off its piers and deposited it in the St. John River. The provincial government's Departmental Building is at the centre. Beside its west entrance is a unique brass plate that indicates water level. The Departmental Building was constructed in 1888-1889 to house a number of government offices. Two thousand tons of stone and three hundred thousand bricks were used, and slate was chosen for the roof.

## 9. Waterloo Row during the 1936 flood

On March 19, as ice jams upriver from Fredericton broke, great volumes of water were released, only to be held back by jams at the railway bridge and near Oromocto. Water levels rose at a rate of four to twelve inches an hour, finally reaching 30 feet, four feet higher than in the 1887 flood. The demolition of the bridge allowed water levels to drop overnight, and this was what school children (for whom classes were cancelled the next day) and other sight-seers witnessed on March 20: toppled utility poles, mountains of ice in the west end of the city, and huge blocks of ice, 16 to 18 inches thick, on Queen Street and Waterloo Row and as far back as Brunswick Street. Property damage amounted to two million dollars.

Chapter 13

# Memorials and Cemeteries

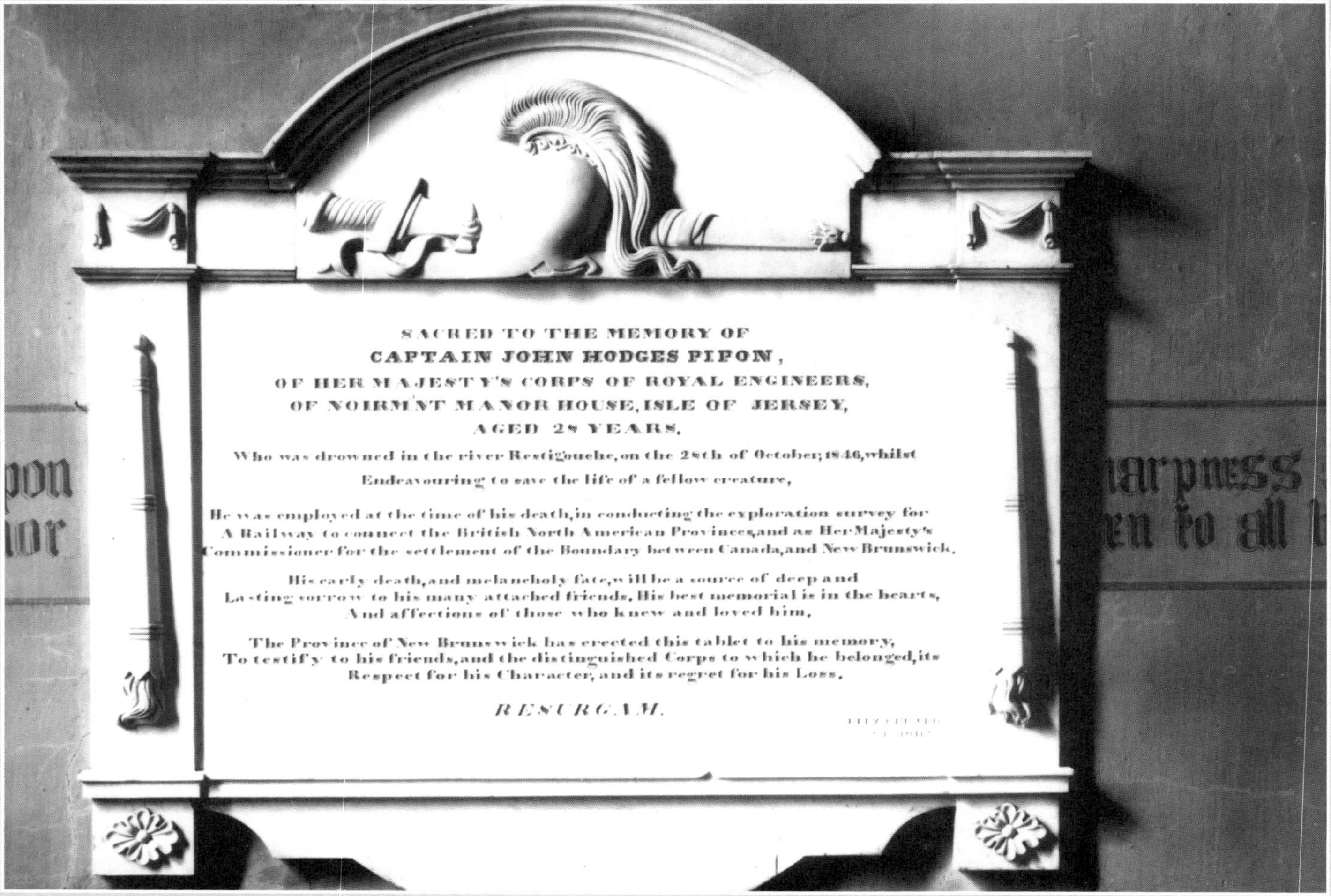

The memorial plaque at Christ Church Parish Church in memory of Captain John Hodges Pipon of Her Majesty's Corps of Royal Engineers. Pipon drowned at age 28 on October 28, 1846 in the Restigouche River, in northern New Brunswick, while conducting a railway survey. He was interred in the Old Burying Ground in Fredericton.

The Robert Burns monument, unveiled on Thanksgiving Day, October 18, 1906, near the B & B Club on the Green. The Fredericton Society of St. Andrews undertook the project and the necessary fundraising. Cast in Scotland by Edinburgh sculptor Alexander Nasmyth, the statue is ten and one-half feet tall and weighs 3,300 pounds. It shows Burns in a natural position, holding a book in one hand and a pen in the other. There was a defect in the casting of the statue, and it had to be returned to Scotland. A replacement statue was installed in September 1911. Mooney & Sons of Saint John installed the six-foot-deep foundation. The statue rests on a ten-foot-square, twelve-foot-high pedestal of gray granite, cut by the Stanstead Granite Quarries Company of Quebec. Three bronze panels, standing out in relief on three sides of the plinth, depict illustrations from three of Burns' most popular poems; a tracing of the name BURNS is cut in a panel on the fourth base.

The Citizens' War Memorial, at the intersection of Queen, King, and Church streets, unveiled on November 11, 1923. The dedicatory ceremony was addressed by Sir John Douglas Hazen, a former mayor of Fredericton and former premier of New Brunswick. The memorial was erected at a cost of $12,000; City Council made a grant of $6,000, and citizens, societies, and organizations readily and heartily subscribed the rest. The white granite monument has a 14-foot shaft surmounted on a 26-ton die, the latter said to be one of the largest blocks of cut granite in Canada. The coat of arms of the city of Fredericton and that of the province of New Brunswick are engraved on the elegant capstone of the 25-foot-high monument. Located directly in front is the cenotaph, an empty granite tomb with a rifle, side arms, and shell helmet on top; a large granite cross stands at the head. Behind the cross, on the front face of the die, is a bronze tablet bearing the names of the 109 Fredericton soldiers who died in World War One. The names of the battles in which they died are inscribed on the four sides of the shaft. In later years, similar bronze tablets were added to honour Fredericton military personnel who gave their lives in World War Two and the Korean War, as well as the merchant mariners who perished in all three conflicts.

## 4. The Armistice Day ceremony at the Citizens' War Memorial and Cenotaph

November 11, 1932

Left to right: John Forrester, Seymour Tyler; Fred Crawford, bandsman in rear; Israel Smith; Ross Fisher, Frank Spencer, and Tom Lynch, bandsmen, in rear; Morris Oldenberg; Karl Walker and Harry Lynch in rear; Bobby Lyons; Martin Horncastle in rear; Ernest Tims, George Gray.

Seymour Tyler became a veteran of two world wars, enlisting in the Canadian Army in 1915. When World War Two broke out, Bugle-Sergeant Tyler went overseas with the Carleton-York Regiment, having already been awarded the Silver Bugle. He also distinguished himself as an honoured member of the black community in New Brunswick for the work he did to promote the pride, unity, and dignity of his race through education.

## 5. The unveiling of the Loyalist Memorial
October 8, 1933

The York-Sunbury Historical Society unveiled the Loyalist Memorial, a bronze tablet on a large native granite boulder, to mark the 150th anniversary—to the day, according to the records of one of the original settlers—of the arrival of the United Empire Loyalists in what was to become Fredericton. The monument was placed close to the small cemetery where some of those who did not survive that first cold winter were buried.

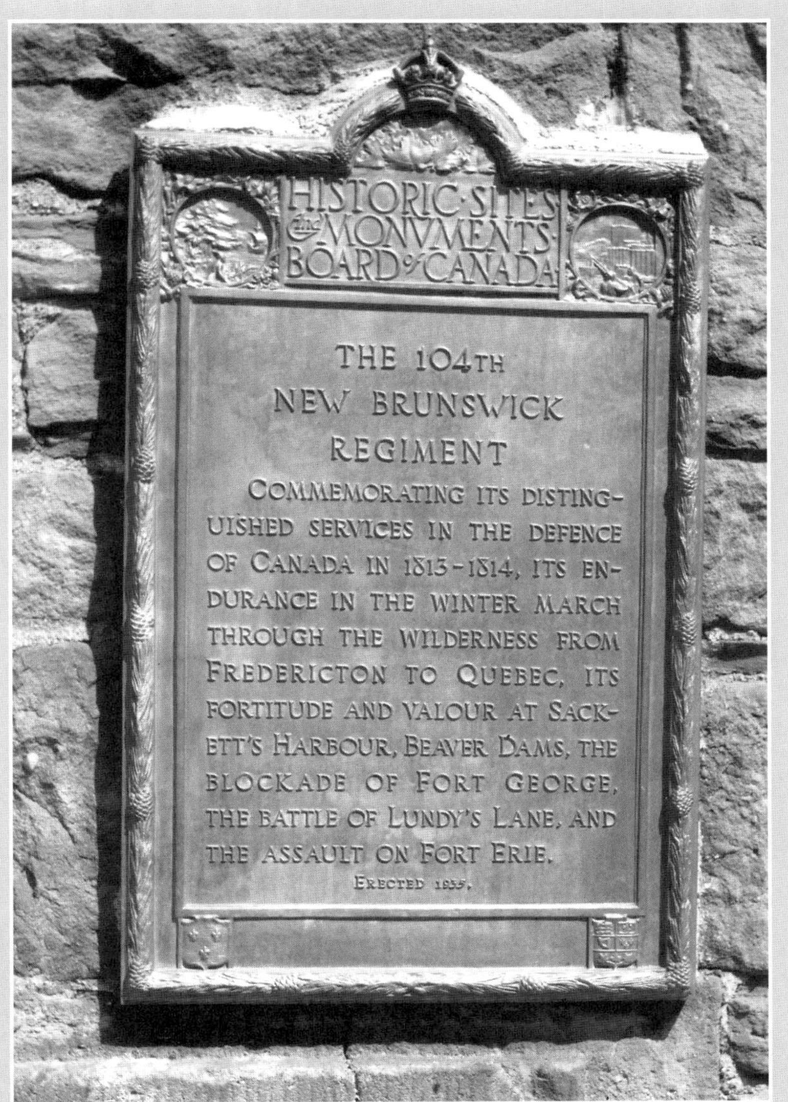


The original memorial plaque to the 104th Regiment. In 1935, the Historic Sites & Monuments Board, through the efforts of the York-Sunbury Historical Society, erected a cairn and plaque to commemorate the historic showshoe march of the 104th New Brunswick Regiment from Fredericton to Quebec City in 1813, to defend the British colonies from American invasion during the War of 1812. The monument was placed at the intersection of Brunswick, King, and Smythe streets, from where the march is believed to have departed. The original plaque mentioned only the first half of the trek. When a new plaque was placed on the wall of the Soldiers' Barracks on Queen Street years later, it added the information that the regiment marched another 350 miles to reach Fort Henry at Kingston, Ontario, making the feat even more remarkable.

## 7. The memorial plaque to Dr. William F. Roberts

The memorial plaque erected by the Historic Sites and Monuments Board in 1939 to honour Dr. William F. Roberts. As a member of the New Brunswick Cabinet, in 1918 Dr. Roberts placed before the legislature a bill to establish a Ministry of Health. His efforts were successful, the department was set up, and he became its first minister. The timing of the legislation was very fortunate, as the province was better able to deal with the Spanish influenza epidemic that broke out that fall.

New Brunswick was the first place in the British Empire to establish a Ministry of Health, and the benefits were so great that the idea was copied in other parts of Canada and the Empire.

This monument in front of the Legislative Building is now shared with plaques honouring Lemuel Allan Wilmot, Charles Fisher, and Sir Howard Douglas.

# 8. The funeral of Captain W.G. Hawkins

1863

The funeral of Captain Walter Godwin Hawkins of Her Majesty's 15th Regiment of Foot, at the Old Burying Ground between Brunswick and George streets, on May 30, 1863. Hawkins, who died suddenly at age 27 after a brief illness, had been well respected for his fine character and bearing. He had served seven years in the 15th Regiment, which was very popular with Frederictonians. While the funeral procession was in progress, stores were closed. The funeral was conducted by Rev. C.G. Coster, and included a Masonic tribute and a military ceremony. The smoke near the grave site was from the guns being fired. The Regimental Band played at the service, returning in silence from the grave. It was announced that the band would not perform in public until June 9, out of respect for Captain Hawkins.

## 9. The Old Burying Ground

c.1867-1869, with the Methodist church in the background

This parcel of land south of Brunswick Street and bounded on the west by Allen Street (later Sunbury Street) and on the east by Barrack Lane (next to the early Park Barracks) was originally intended as a park. However, a burial place was needed, so the four and one-half acres were granted to the Church of England as "the graveyard," later called the"Old Public Burial Ground." The first formal interment took place there in 1787, although there may have been some unrecorded burials earlier. In 1878 the cemetery became the responsibility of the city, which decided in 1886 to impose a limit on further interments. A notice was published in the local newspapers that year to restrict future burials to those who declared their right of possession to clearly specified lots by October 1, 1886, and that right was exercised until the mid-twentieth century.

## 10. The gravestone of Bliss Carman

The gravestone of Bliss Carman, near that of his cousin Charles G.D. Roberts, in the Forest Hill Cemetery. The province of New Brunswick erected the distinctive, gray granite tombstone, on the back of which is Carman's own modest epitaph, from one of his poems:

*Have little care that life is brief/ And less that art is long/ Success is in the silences/ Though fame is in the song.*

In accordance with the poet's wishes as expressed in his poem "The Grave Tree," the University of New Brunswick planted a maple seedling at his gravesite several years later.

## 11. The gravestone of Sir Charles G.D. Roberts, in the Forest Hill Cemetery

The epitaph on Sir Charles Roberts' gravestone is a stanza from his poem "The Summons," first published in *New Poems* (1919):

*Up, Soul and out*
*Into the deeps alone*
*To the long peal*
*and the shout*
*Of those trumpets*
*Blown and blown*

A holograph manuscript of *New Poems* is held at the University of New Brunswick Archives. The gravestone was erected by Elsie Pomeroy, Roberts' close friend, secretary, and official biographer.

Chapter 14

# Panoramic Views

## 1. Fredericton as seen from the top of Exhibition Palace

To the right of the palace dome (lower left corner) is the wooden Brunswick Street Baptist church, and in the centre background is the Methodist church. In the centre foreground is the two-storey, oblong Baptist Seminary and, to the right, George Street Baptist church and the Auld Kirk (in its original location).

## 2. A view from the Methodist church tower

A view from the tower of the Methodist church (later Wilmot United Church), looking north toward the St. Mary's shore. The Soldiers' Barracks is at the far left in the centre of the photograph. To the right of the barracks is the stone Guard House, with its pillars. Just beyond is the former Militia Arms Store, a wooden building constructed in 1832 to house military weapons and ammunition; visible in this photo is the addition made to the rear of the building so it could be used as a military hospital. The long building nearest the river is the Drill Hall. A double row of ice-breaking piers protected the wooden highway bridge on the upriver side. To the right of the bridge is the Post Office and Customs Building (later the John Thurston Clark Memorial Building), and in the right foreground is the office of *The Farmer* newspaper.

## 3. A view looking northwest from the Methodist church tower

A view looking northwest from the tower of the Methodist (Wilmot) church, with one of the decorative turrets in the lower left foreground. Power lines run between the rows of closely built houses, many of them with ladders on their roofs for fire protection. The city was plagued by fires, a serious matter in a community with so many wooden structures, where sparks and flames could readily jump from one building to another. The major blaze of 1850 began in a barn next door to this church. In the background, along Queen Street, from the left are the Randolph Building, City Hall, and the first normal school.

## 4. A view looking west from the Legislative Building c.1880

The Methodist church is at centre, and *The Morning Star* office is clearly identified to the right, at Regent and Queen streets. This newspaper was published from 1878 to 1879, and as *The Star* from 1879 to 1880.

## 5. A view, from the roof of City Hall, of the south side of Queen Street

The signs for Manchester House (near the centre), Albion House (dry goods), and F. McPeake's dry goods store are visible among the numerous businesses. The Methodist (Wilmot) church stands in the background. The trees in the foreground show why Fredericton has been called the city of stately elms.

# Image Sources

Almost all the photographs are from the collections of the Provincial Archives of New Brunswick, identified by the prefix "PANB." "P5/" identifies photos from the George Taylor collection; "P11/" photos are those of Isaac Erb; "P14/" is for Harvey Studios; "P15/" is the Fredericton Fire Department; "P42/" pictures are from the album of the 22nd Cheshire Regiment; and "P120/" identifies the Madge Smith collection. "P37/," "P61/," and "P194/" photos have miscellaneous sources, and "P44/" photos are from the National Archives of Canada.

Several photographs are from the York-Sunbury Historical Society, identified as "P4/2/" or "P132/" for those in the provincial archives and "YSM" for those from the society's museum.

The small number of pictures from outside sources are identified individually.

### Cover

YSM

### Introduction

PANB MC375
PANB P11/42
PANB P5/414

### Chapter 1: Military Compound

1. PANB P42/75
2. PANB P42/76
3. PANB P42/77
4. PANB P37/345
5. PANB P11/44
6. PANB P5/741
7. PANB P5/239
8. PANB P44/25541
9. PANB P5/66
10. PANB P5/151
11. PANB P5/712
12. PANB P5/378
13. PANB P5/368
14. PANB P11/46
15. PANB P37/164
16. PANB P37/385
17. PANB P37/109
18. PANB P37/110

### Chapter 2: Government

1. PANB P5/310
2. PANB P5/41
3. PANB P44/25573
4. PANB P194/221
5. PANB P194/4
6. PANB P14/4
7. PANB P37/162
8. PANB P5/165
9. PANB P33/45

### Chapter 3: Celestial City

1. PANB P11/39
2. PANB P5/281
3. PANB P36/41
4. PANB P120/3/62
5. PANB P120/3/38
6. PANB P120/3/43
7. Courtesy Harvey Studios
8. PANB P120/3/87
9. PANB P120/3/57
10. PANB P5/305A
11. PANB P37/170
12. PANB P5/307
13. PANB P5/895
14. PANB P120/3/30
15. PANB P5/274
16. PANB P120/3/31

### Chapter 4: Education

1. PANB P5/87
2. PANB P120/1/46
3. PANB P5/327
4. PANB P5/92
5. Courtesy Harvey Studios
6. Courtesy Pearle Ross estate
7. PANB P47/6
8. PANB P11/149
9. PANB P37/546
10. PANB P120/2/21
11. PANB P11/47
12. PANB P5/297
13. PANB P5/243
14. YSM (also PANB P132/139)
15. YSM (also PANB P132/125)

### Chapter 5: Public Buildings

1. PANB P11/48
2. PANB P5/356
3. PANB P5/59
4. PANB P270/7
5. PANB P5/43
6. PANB P5/167
7. PANB P1/5
8. PANB P5/298
9. PANB P11/50
10. Courtesy Harvey Studios
11. PANB P61/426
12. PANB P32/128
13. PANB P15/13
14. PANB P15/24
15. PANB P5/374
16. PANB P15/31
17. PANB P350/184

### Chapter 6: Businesses

1. PANB P5/289
2. PANB P37/159
3. PANB P14/41
4. PANB P270/4
5. PANB P5/357
6. Courtesy Harvey Studios
7. YSM (also PANB P132/131)
8. YSM (also PANB P132/135)
9. PANB P5/422
10. PANB P5/340
11. PANB P5/405A
12. PANB P5/342
13. PANB P5/448
14. PANB P5/426
15. PANB P194/385

16. Courtesy Glen Boyce (also PANB P194/466)
17. YSM (also PANB P132/130)
18. PANB P5/302
19. PANB P5/423
20. YSM (also PANB P132/129)
21. PANB P5/107
22. PANB P11/79
23. YSM (also PANB P132/133)

## Chapter 7: Street Scenes

1. PANB P5/222
2. PANB P5/22
3. PANB P5/238
4. PANB P44/25555
5. PANB P5/291
6. PANB P5/386
7. YSM (also PANB P132/122)
8. PANB P5/221
9. PANB P406/32

## Chapter 8: Historic Homes and People

1. PANB P5/17
2. PANB P412/25
3. PANB P120/18/25
4. PANB P5/294
5. PANB P5/882
6. PANB P5/860
7. PANB P5/228
8. PANB P5/287
9. PANB P5/292
10. PANB P5/738
11. PANB P5/550
12. PANB P5/296
13. PANB P5/88
14. PANB P5/110
15. PANB P5/293B
16. PANB P32/4
17. PANB P120/18/28
18. PANB P120/18/22
19. PANB P5/141
20. PANB P1/3
21. YSM

## Chapter 9: Social Life

1. Courtesy Harvey Studios
2. PANB P270/8
3. PANB P37/487/1
4. PANB P5/317
5. PANB P5/324
6. PANB P5/279
7. PANB P459/1
8. PANB P15/26
9. PANB P37/257
10. PANB P14/78
11. PANB P14/15
12. Courtesy Harvey Studios
13. PANB P5/247
14. PANB P42/55
15. PANB P5/395B
16. PANB P42/63
17. PANB P58/53
18. PANB P4/2/0133

## Chapter 10: Transportation and Visitors

1. *Illustrated London News*
2. PANB P37/238
3. PANB P37/95
4. PANB P60/81
5. PANB P5/314
6. PANB P5/117
7. PANB P5/373
8. PANB P4/2/0105
9. PANB P5/216
10. PANB P5/275
11. PANB P104/10
12. PANB P14/70
13. PANB P14/71
14. PANB P37/503
15. PANB P264/11

## Chapter 11: Hotels

1. YSM (also PANB P132/128)
2. PANB P37/166
3. PANB P14/24
4. PANB P5/478
5. PANB P5/56
6. PANB P61/474
7. PANB P61/473
8. Courtesy Harvey Studios

## Chapter 12: Floods

1. PANB P15/16
2. PANB P5/283
3. PANB P5/316
4. PANB P4/2/07
5. PANB P5/315
6. PANB P11/63
7. PANB P14/76
8. PANB P14/75
9. PANB P14/74

## Chapter 13: Memorials and Cemeteries

1. PANB P5/86
2. PANB P18/261
3. PANB P120/1/63
4. YSM (also PANB P132/123)
5. YSM
6. PANB P272/5
7. PANB P107/41
8. PANB P37/246
9. PANB P42/62
10. PANB P120/1/68
11. Courtesy Ted Jones

## Chapter 14: Panoramic Views

1. PANB P4/1/2
2. PANB P5/290B
3. PANB P5/285
4. PANB P5/161
5. PANB P5/231

## Back Cover:

PANB P120/1/36